101 ESL Activities, Games, and Resources for Teaching English Online

Jackie Bolen

(www.eslactivity.org)

Table of Contents

About the Author: Jackie Bolen

I taught English in South Korea for a decade to every level and type of student. I've taught every age from kindergarten kids to adults. Most of my time centered around teaching at two universities: five years at a science and engineering school out in the rice paddies of Chungcheongnam-Do, and four years at a major university in Busan where I taught high level classes for students majoring in English. I now teach ESL/EFL students in Vancouver, Canada. In my spare time, you can usually find me outside surfing, biking, hiking, or on the hunt for the most delicious kimchi I can find. It's not so easy in Vancouver!

In case you were wondering what my academic qualifications are, I hold a Master of Arts Degree in Psychology. During my time in Korea I successfully completed both the Cambridge CELTA and DELTA certification programs. With the combination of ten years teaching ESL/EFL learners of all ages and levels, and the more formal teaching qualifications I obtained, I have a solid foundation on which to offer teaching advice. I truly hope that you find this book useful and would love it if you sent me an email with any questions or feedback that you might have.

Jackie Bolen around the Internet

ESL Speaking (www.eslactivity.org)

Jackie Bolen (www.jackiebolen.com)

Twitter: @bolen_jackie

Email: jb.business.online@gmail.com

You may also want to check out some of other books on Amazon (search for Jackie Bolen), but here are a few of my most popular titles:

39 No-Prep/Low-Prep ESL Speaking Activities

39 Awesome 1-1 ESL Activities

101 ESL Activities for Teenagers and Adults

Life After ESL: Foreign Teachers Returning Home

How to Use this Book

Teaching English online is in some ways quite similar to teaching in a classroom but also different. The main thing is that most online teachers teach students 1-1 instead of in a classroom setting with up to 40 students. This means that activities and games have to be chosen carefully with this in mind. Something like "talk with a partner" or group activities like an English scavenger hunt simply won't work.

That said, there are LOTS of things to do with students when teaching online that involve more than just powering through a textbook page by page or "free-talking." Using a variety of interesting, engaging and student-centred activities can go a long ways towards retaining students and helping them improve their English skills. If you have some freedom to design your own online English lessons (some platforms require you to use their materials), then this book is for you.

You'll find some general tips for teaching English online, including some recommendations for online teaching platforms to consider as well as tech tips and more. Then, you'll find dozens of activities designed specially for online English teaching. They are organized into various sections, from listening to reading, icebreakers to multi-skill activities, etc. so you should be able to find what you're looking for quickly and easily. Finally, there are ten of the best resources to consider for lesson plans, worksheets, puzzles and more.

It's the most comprehensive guide to activities and games for teaching English online. I hope you'll find it useful when preparing some great online lessons for your students.

20 Tips for Teaching English Online

If you're just getting started with online English teaching, then check out these tips and tricks for doing it well. After that, you'll find the activities, games and resources.

#1: Consider Specializing

It's possible to make a living teaching ESL online as a jack-of-all-trades. However, you may also want to consider specializing in just a few things. For example, the IELTS exam, business English or English job interviews. You'll be able to give your students a great learning experience and may find that lots of referrals come your way if you do it well.

#2: Ask Students What they Want

One of the best tips for how to teach English, whether online or offline is to ask students what they want to work on with you. Their answers will sometimes be very different from what you might think.

For online teaching, many will say that they want to work on free-talking or conversation for at least part of the class. Others may want to improve their reading skills or get a higher score on an English proficiency exam. Finally, some may be preparing for an English job interview or to travel. The way we teach these students varies greatly and so knowing what students want to learn is important for making decisions about how and what to teach.

#3: Become Familiar With English Proficiency Exams

There are lots of students who want help preparing for a specific English exam like TOEIC, TOEFL or IELTS. If you can specialize in one or more of these and get your students some serious results, you'll have students lining up to learn from you!

However, something to keep in mind is that these kinds of students are usually for the short-term and will discontinue the classes once their exam is done.

#4: Talk about Expectations with your Student

When asked for tips about how to teach English online, many teachers mention the necessity of talking with student before beginning to set the expectations both parties have of each other. For example, you might want to talk about:

- Cancellation policy

- Payment

- Homework

- Types of activities

- Assessment

It's also wise to regularly check in regularly with students as the class progresses. They'll often have helpful feedback about what they'd like to change and also what's working for them.

#5: Students Come and Students Go

Teaching online requires a bit of a thick skin. Some students will stick with you for years while others will stay for only a very short time.

In some cases, students had a very short-term goal like preparing for an English proficiency exam or an English job interview. However, others may find another tutor that they like better. This is okay and a normal part of the online teaching experience so don't dwell too much on it.

That said, if you're constantly losing students and having a difficult time filling your schedule, reflect a bit more deeply on this. If possible, get a recording of yourself teaching and ask a trusted colleague to review it and offer some feedback.

#6: Invest in some Good Equipment

Trying to teach English online with crappy equipment is an exercise in frustration! At the very minimum, be sure to have:

- A good desk and comfortable chair

- High quality camera and headset/microphone

- Nice background

- Small whiteboard with markers

Don't forget to have a backup option. Headsets and microphones are especially prone to failing at some point in time so have your old pair at the ready just in case. It's far better than having to cancel a class due to this technology fail!

#7: Manage Time Well

Another tip for how to teach ESL online is to manage time well. Stay organized and be sure to give yourself enough time to prepare for classes, evaluate tests or homework and rest too.

If at all possible, try to schedule blocks of classes with small breaks in between instead of an hour here and an hour there. This will allow time for a social life too!

#8: Have Some Fun

Just because you're on your 10th, 30 minute class that day doesn't mean that the student is! It's probably their only session. Yawning, frowning and looking bored certainly won't get you more booked classes so be peppy and upbeat and if you're not feeling it, take a break for a day or two or consider teaching fewer classes.

Be encouraging as well! Praise even small improvements regularly.

#9: Be Prepared

When teaching any sort of ESL class, preparation is required! Have at least a basic lesson plan as teaching English is more than just chatting with the student. If you only do this, students will soon wonder what exactly they're paying for and their English ability may not really improve that much!

#10: Don't Forget About Assessment

Good teachers regularly assess how their students are doing in order to tailor their lessons more specifically. This is especially easy to do in a 1-1 TEFL class.

Almost all students have a weakness or two among the following things:

- speaking

- pronunciation

- listening

- reading

- writing

- vocabulary

- grammar

- Etc.

There are certainly formal assessment tools, but most teachers will be able to figure this out over a few sessions with a student. For example, maybe the student has a difficult time using irregular verbs in the past, reads extremely slowly and uses very limited vocabulary.

#11: Consider Various Online Teaching Platforms

There are a number of online teaching platforms to consider which can help make the transition into teaching online easier. You'll get a feel for how it works and pick up a few tips and tricks along the way without having to organize everything yourself.

But, not all online teaching platforms are created equal and of course, each of them have their pros and cons. Another consideration is that not all teachers will accepted to all of them so be sure to apply for 3, 4 or even more. Some of the best ones to consider are the following:

- *Verbling*

- *First Tutors*

- *Take Lessons*

- *Preply*

- *VIPKID*

- *Italki*

- *Amazing Talker*

- *DaDaABC*

- *QKids*

- *iTutorGroup*

- *GogoKid*

- *51Talk*

- *EnglishHunt*

Readers—I know that you may want me to tell you which one is the "best." However, there is no one single option that will work well for all teachers. Some of the factors to consider are the following:

- Who is hiring

- Minimum qualifications required

- Rate of pay

- Student locations and hours of work

- Minimum hours

- Materials provided or not

- Age of students

- Etc.

As you can see, there are a lot of factors to think about! Do your research to find the online teaching platform that will work for you.

A quick tip is to teach on at least two of them. Although it can take a bit more work to coordinate schedules and payments between the two, it's a protection in case one of them goes under so you're not left entirely without income. These online teaching platforms are often newer companies and may, or may not do well.

#12: Or, Venture Out on your Own

Another option to consider for online English teaching is to teach without the support of one of the companies mentioned above. The main reason to consider this is that you'll get to keep all the money instead of a percentage of it. However, you'll have to do all the work of scheduling, managing payments and finding students.

If you're tech-savvy and can manage creating a website or other platform to promote yourself, organized enough to manage bookings and are considering online teaching for the long-term, it may certainly be worth it.

#13: How to Teach ESL Online—All About No-Shows

One of the most annoying things about teaching English online is to deal with no-shows. Have a firm but fair policy that you explain to the student before getting started and stick to it. If you're using one of the online platforms, they'll likely already have this policy in place.

#14: Consider Zoom Instead of Skype

A few years ago, everyone was using *Skype* for online teaching. However, these days, *Zoom* seems to be more popular as the connection is more stable and it's more hassle-free. If you haven't tried it out yet, it's free for a 1-1 lesson and a few bucks for the ability to host sessions with more than one student.

#15: Repetition and Review

When people ask me how to teach English, online or offline, one of the first things I tell them is to not forget about review! This is key for students to retain what they're learning. Review throughout the lesson, at the end of the lesson and then at the beginning of the next class.

#16: Consider Using Props

A nice tip for how to teach English online is to consider using some props, especially with kids. Have some puppets for example and do your best to bring them to life. This will help students to pay close attention to what's going on.

#17: Don't Forget about the Parents if You're Teaching Kids

If you're teaching English online to kids, remember who is paying the bill! You'll want to do your best to keep in touch with parents and provide feedback about how the lessons are going with their children.

#18: Close all Other Screens on your Computer and Put your Phone on Silent

Let's be real here for a second. There's almost nothing worse than someone who is checking Facebook or their email or texting a friend during an online English class! Close all other screens and turn your phone on silent so that you can focus on the lesson.

Even if a student is taking a minute or two to read something or do some written work, stay focused and don't let your mind wander!

#19: Keep Track of your Lessons

Whatever method you use to keep track of lesson topics, homework, payments, etc. use it! Relying on memory for something like this is a recipe for disaster even if with only 1 or 2 students.

Imagine showing up for a class and pulling out the same lesson plan you did last month? The student will know for sure and will almost always point this out. Then you'll be left scrambling at the last second. We've all been there but it's easy to avoid.

#20: Mute your Microphone if You're Going to Type a Lot

Keyboards are usually very loud in someone's ear. Be sure to press mute when typing more than a few words.

Speaking Focused Activities

If you ask students what they want to work on with you, most of them will say speaking or conversation. With that in mind, here are some of the best options to get your students talking!

120-90-60

Time: 5-10 minutes

Level: Intermediate-Advanced

Materials Required: None

If you want to help students speak fluently, this is the perfect speaking activity. Give students a topic that they know a lot about. For example: good or bad points about their school or hometown. Give them two minutes to prepare, depending on their level. But, emphasize that they should just write one or two words for each point, and not full sentences because it is actually a speaking activity and not a writing one.

Then the student has to give their speech and talk continuously for two minutes, while you listen. I use an online stopwatch so that students can see the clock count down.

After that, the student has to repeat the activity except that they have to include ALL the same information as before, just in 90 seconds. Then do it again with 60 more seconds. One way that you can help students make the transition to less time is by giving them 30 seconds between rounds to think about how to say something more concisely, go over in their head the part of their speech where they had to slow down for some reason or to think about where they could use conjunctions.

For lower level students, you can adjust the times to make them shorter and easier because talking for two minutes can be quite difficult.

Emphasize that students must include all of the key information even though they have less time to say it. Speak more quickly or more concisely!

Teaching Tips:

It can be really difficult to find good speaking activities that are focused on fluency instead of accuracy, but this is an excellent one and I try to use it a couple of times per semester.

Emphasize to your students that they must include all the same information they spoke the first time, so they'll either have to say things more concisely or speak faster. Present it as a difficult, but attainable challenge that they can achieve. At the end of the second and third rounds, ask your students how much they were able to include as a percentage. If they did well, tell them to pat themselves on the back for achieving something that wasn't easy. A small motivational moment in your class!

It's a good idea to remind your students that spoken speech is more informal than written discourse, particularly in the areas of sentence length and connectors. When we write, things like "however," "although," and "moreover" are common but in spoken speech we mostly just use simple connectors like "and," "but," and "or." Also, in spoken discourse the length of an utterance is much shorter and we don't need to use complicated grammatical constructions.

Procedure:

1. Give the student a topic and some time to prepare their "speech."

2. The student gives their speech, talking for two minutes without stopping.

3. He/she gives their speech again, this time in 90 seconds. And then another time in 60 seconds.

4. Optionally, the teacher can ask some follow-up questions based on what the student said.

Conversation Starters

Time: 5 minutes

Level: Intermediate-Advanced

Materials Required: Conversation starters

These are 10 conversation starters which are guaranteed to generate some interesting conversations. They make a nice warm-up activity at the beginning of a lesson. Or, a topic for "free-talking" time if you include that in your online English lessons.

If I Won the Lottery

Describe what you would do or what you would buy if you won the lotto. I usually specify an amount of $1,000,000.

Bucket List

Think of five things you want to do before you die.

Guilty Pleasures

Explain to the student what a guilty pleasure is—they likely won't know. Then, it's time for confessions!

Things You've Learned Lately

Think of two or three things that you couldn't do as a child but can do now. Emphasize that it's related to a skill of some kind or you'll just get answers like drinking or smoking.

Last Purchase

Talk about the last thing you bought that was more than $100.

You're the President

Talk about what you top three priorities would be if you were in office.

Favorite Things

Each of you makes three questions with the starter, "What is your favorite _____." Then, discuss them.

Horoscopes

Find some daily or monthly horoscopes online. Read their description and see if they match.

People in Your Life

Who are the three people that you spend the most time with these days?

The Best Decision

Think of a difficult decision you've made, but about which you're confident you made the right choice.

Flashcard Sentences

Time: 5 minutes

Level: Beginner-Intermediate

Materials Required: Flashcards

You can use this for whatever grammar and vocabulary points you're teaching. Pull a flashcard with a picture of a vocabulary word on it from your pile and the student makes a sentence with that card. A correct sentence gets the card. If incorrect, the teacher keeps the card. The winner is the person with the most flashcards.

For absolute beginners, it's possible to adapt this activity and have the student just say the word.

Procedure:

1. Take a flashcard from your pile.

2. Ask the student to make a sentence with that card.

3. If correct, the student keeps the card (virtually!).

4. If incorrect, the teacher keeps the card. Continue until the cards are gone, one of you has a certain number of points (three or five), or the time is up.

If I Had a Million Dollars

Time: 20 minutes

Level: Intermediate-Advanced

Materials Required: If I Had a Million Dollars song by the Barenaked Ladies

This is an activity to discuss hypothetical situations and to focus on conditionals. You can start by playing the Barenaked Ladies song or video of the same name. Then, tell the student that there is a big Lotto drawing coming up, you have a ticket and are thinking about what you'll do if you win. Give the student a minute to think about what they'd do with the money. Then, have a discussion about your ideas. You could start in the reverse with the Lotto ticket scenario and then play the song after. It's up to you!

If you want to challenge your advanced level students, find the song lyrics, cut and paste them into a worksheet, but omit some of the vocabulary words and get students to fill in the blanks as they listen to the song. I find that one blank out of every 15-20 words is a good rule of thumb.

Procedure:

1. Set up the scenario for the student: a big Lotto drawing is coming up and you each have a ticket. Give your student a couple of minutes to think about what they'd do with the money. Then, have a short discussion about your ideas.

2. Play the Barenaked Ladies song. I use a YouTube version with lyrics. Optionally, have students fill in a worksheet with some of the song lyric words omitted.

3. Optional: further work on conditionals, including a full lesson, worksheet, etc.

I'm an Alien

Time: 5 minutes

Level: Beginner-Advanced

Materials Required: None

Begin by telling the student that you are an alien. You landed just a few minutes earlier, right outside their home. Since you are new here, you don't know a lot of words, and you need some help.

You can create a mission scenario and elicit vocabulary that will help you. Maybe you want to send a letter telling your mother you arrived safely. You can elicit words like pen, paper, stamp, envelope, or post office. Maybe you need to meet someone in another part of the city, such as the library. You can elicit locations as well as direction words.

Procedure:

1. Tell the student that you are an alien an that you need some help.

2. Create a mission scenario and elicit vocabulary that will help you complete it. For example, you want to send a letter telling your mother you arrived safely. You can elicit words like pen, paper, stamp, envelop, and post office.

3. Give the student a chance to be the alien, if you would like to extend the activity.

Making Videos

Time: 1-5 hours

Level: Beginner-Advanced

Materials Required: Smartphone and/or computer

For my conversation classes, I rarely give students written homework. It doesn't really make sense and it seems far better to me that my students have to practice speaking. Plus, at least in Korea, everybody loves using their Smartphone so this gives my students another excuse to do this!

I base the homework on whatever I'm teaching. For example, in one of my higher level classes we were talking about good and bad manners, so I had my students choose a specific situation (going to someone's home, at a coffee shop, eating out, etc.) and explain what things you should and shouldn't do. For lower level students, I've done things like getting students to introduce themselves and then giving a few topics that they have to cover such as family, hobbies and hopes for the future. Students have to film themselves talking about these things.

It's really easy for the students to upload the videos on *YouTube* and then send the link so you can watch and evaluate them. To make it even more fun for the students, I tell them that they can make the video with someone else if they wish. If it's a person in the same class, the requirements are usually slightly higher (for example, five minutes instead of three). But, they could also do it with anybody outside the class. I've had students get their families, little brothers or sisters, girlfriends or boyfriends, international students they know in their dormitory and even random people on the street to help them. It's usually really funny and interesting and it's homework that I truly don't mind grading.

Teaching Tips:

Getting your students to make videos is a particularly effective way to work on functional language or language sub-skills. Some things you could focus on for solo videos include: giving an opinion, offering advice, using more or less formal language depending on the situation, marking the main points of a discourse through emphasis, and verbal cues or transition statements. If there are two or more people, you can focus on the things previously mentioned but could also consider making a request, apologizing, agreeing, disagreeing, asking for an opinion, turn-taking skills, initiating, etc.

What you choose to focus on depends on the topic you choose and whether the student is alone or with a partner. For example, in solo speech it can be really useful to focus on something like grammatical accuracy, pronunciation or intonation. However, in a pair your students could work on offering advice, or transition statements.

Even if you're not stellar at using technology, chances are that your students mostly are, especially if they are teenagers or university students so don't let this hinder you. I've found that even the mature students in my classes could figure it out, usually by asking their own teenagers or students (many of them are teachers themselves.) Of course, you should put up your own video on *YouTube* first so you at least have a basic idea of the process. If students are having particular problems, I recommend instructing them to Google it in their own language because the question has surely been answered already.

I never give additional points or take away points for things like poor sound or lighting quality as long as I can see and hear them. I instead focus on English use, since it's an English class and not a video making or editing one. That said, if a student uses their creative powers and goes above and beyond what the other students have done, I'll usually give them a bonus point or two.

Some students worry about privacy issues so I always mention that I'll grade the videos very quickly (within a day) and as soon as they get an email from me with my comment, they can delete the video. Another option is to have students send you the video itself by email or upload it to a shared *Google Drive* or *DropBox* account.

Procedure:

1. Decide on the criteria for the video: alone/partner/group, length, topic, etc.
2. Explain the criteria very clearly to your students and have them work on it for homework.
3. Students can upload the video to *YouTube* and then send the link to the teacher.

Memory Tray

Time: 5-10 minutes

Level: Beginner-Intermediate

Materials Required: A tray with several items/PowerPoint/whiteboard

Before class, prepare a tray with 10-20 items, depending on the age of the students. Keep it covered while you tell the students they will have a short time to study the tray. Give 20 seconds to a minute, depending on their age and the number of items. Make sure the student is able to see the items clearly. You may want to consider using a PowerPoint slide for this. Then, cover the items back up or remove the slide.

Variation 1: Students simply need to list the items they saw.

Variation 2: Students need to recall the location of the items in relation to one another.

Variation 3: Move some of the items around or remove them and students have to tell you what changed.

Procedure:

1. In advance, prepare a tray of 10-20 items (more for older students) or a PowerPoint with images.
2. Tell the student to look carefully at the items.
3. Tell them not to write anything down.
4. Reveal the items for 20-60 seconds, depending on how many items there are.
5. Have the students reconstruct what they saw using one of the variations mentioned above.

Real House Hunters

Time: 10-15 minutes

Level: Intermediate-Advanced

Materials Required: *YouTube* clip of *House Hunters*

If you have never seen *House Hunters* or one of its many spin-offs, it is a show in which a couple looks at three houses before choosing the one they want. After seeing each house, they talk about the good and bad points of each house such as, near a park and/or their school, etc. For this activity, your student will "view" each house, describe it: furniture, colors, condition (new, old, stylish. . .), and give their opinion about it.

Procedure:

1. Begin with a clip of *House Hunters* from *YouTube*.
2. Talk about the kinds of information and issues the house hunters discuss: size and style of the house, necessary repairs, location, etc.
3. You can discuss how the student feels about their own house.

Real Life Role Play

Time: 5-20 minutes

Level: Beginner-Advanced

Materials Required: Variable according to the role play

Depending on your student's individual needs, you can create real-life role plays to help practice situations they may encounter outside of class. If your student is preparing to study overseas, this could include school application interviews, common school situations, or everyday situations, like ordering food at *McDonald's* or talking to a shop clerk. Or, perhaps your student is a doctor or nurse who has to talk to patients in English. Or, a banker who has to make phone calls to English speaking customers.

Choose a specific role play, such as asking a clerk for help finding a shirt in a shop. If possible, go to an actual shop and you play the role of the clerk. Prompt the student to ask you for help finding something, for example a shirt. You could then ask questions to get more information about the shirt they want: size, color, style (tee, button down, polo, etc.). If your student will have an admission interview in English, do some research to get examples of questions and rehearse them together. If you are using a textbook, this could be an excellent extension activity or an alternative to the provided dialogues.

Teaching Tips:

Act inexperienced by asking your student questions for clarification to repeat themselves, etc. to replicate those aspects of real-life conversations.

Procedure:

1. Identify a real-world communication need your student has.

2. Play the role of the person your student will be communicating with. For example, at a shop. Prompt the student to ask you for help finding an item. Ask questions to get more information about the shirt they want: size, color, style (tee, button down, polo, etc.).

3. If using a textbook and/or if your student has no real world communication needs, use the textbook as a springboard for more realistic role plays.

Role-Plays

Time: 10 minutes

Level: Beginner-Advanced

Materials Required: None

Give the students a conversation starter to get them going. For example, if you're talking about *feelings* in class that day, you can use:

A: Hey _____, how are you doing?

B: I'm great, how are you?

A: I'm _____ (sad, embarrassed, angry, bored, etc.). ***Anything besides, "I'm fine, thank you, and you?" is good. ****

B: Oh? What's wrong?

A: _____.

B: _____.

Another context that I often use this activity with is *illness or injury*. For example:

A: Hey _____, you don't look (sound) so good! What's wrong?

B: Oh yeah, I'm not good. I _____.

A: Really? _____.

B: _____.

A: _____.

One final context that I use this with is *excuses*. For example:

A: Hey _____, you're _____ minutes late!

B: I'm really sorry. I've been/I had to _____.

A: Hmmm . . . _____.

Work together to write the conversation with the student. You can adjust the number of lines and how detailed of a starter you give to suit the ability level of your student. For lower level students, it can be helpful to have a word bank on the board relevant to the context so that the writing portion of this activity doesn't get too long (you could also provide them with a detailed, fill in the blank script). Then, memorize the conversation (no papers when speaking!), and do it as a role-play, adding actions, emotions, etc.

I really like this activity because it's perfect for lower level students who want to practice "conversation" but don't quite have the skills to do this on their own and it's also a good way to force your advanced students to use some new grammar or vocabulary that you're teaching.

Teaching Tips:

Having your students make conversations is very useful for practicing functional language and speaking sub-skills. I usually choose one or two functions to mention when I'm giving the instructions for the activity and provide a bit of coaching and language input surrounding that, depending on the level—beginners will need more help.

The functions in particular that fit well with partner conversations include agreeing, disagreeing, apologizing, and asking advice. The sub-skills that you can emphasize are things like turn-taking, initiating a conversation, speaking for an appropriate length of time, stress and intonation, responding (really?), and cohesive devices, particularly noun pronoun reference: A: I saw a <u>movie</u> last night. B: Which <u>one</u> did you see? A. I saw <u>Ironman.</u> It was good.

Procedure:

1. Prepare a conversation starter based on what you are studying.

2. Write the conversation starter on the whiteboard, PowerPoint, or on a handout.

3. Complete the conversation with the student. Then, prepare to speak by memorizing and adding in stress and intonation.

4. Do the entire role-play.

Show and Tell

Time: 5 minutes

Level: Beginner-Advanced

Materials Required: An object

This is a classic activity from way back in elementary school but it can work well in your online ESL classes too. Tell students a few days before the "show and tell" class that they need to bring an object from home that is meaningful to them. This is usually easy because students are usually at home for online classes! If it's something really big (a piano) or something that doesn't transport easily (a cat), then they can take a picture of it on their phone. Or, just move their computer so that you can see if if they're at home.

Students give a short presentation, talking about the item and why it's meaningful to them. The teacher can ask a few follow-up questions. Switch roles and talk about something that's important to you, with the student asking some follow-up questions.

Procedure:

1. Tell students to bring a meaningful object from home, or send a picture if bringing the object isn't practical.

2. Students introduce the object in a short presentation of 1-2 minutes, depending on the level.

3. The teachers listens and asks some follow-up questions. Switch roles.

Test Prep: Describing a Photo

Time: 15 minutes

Level: Intermediate-Advanced

Materials Required: Prepared images and accompanying vocabulary, timer (phone, kitchen timer, etc.)

Optional Materials: Recording device

Some standardized tests of English ability have a speaking task that evaluates how well the test taker can describe a picture. The image may or may not be accompanied by vocabulary the test taker must use in his/her description. Therefore, for this activity you should prepare several images and vocabulary, such as a noun and a preposition or adverb.

Depending on the level of the student, you may want to begin with some useful language, such as:

at the top/bottom

on the left/right

in the corner/middle

"I think/It looks like _____ (is happening.)"

After you have gone over the useful phrases, show a picture to the student and ask him/her what is happening. Set the timer for one minute. Encourage the student to describe it in as much detail as possible. Elicit further elaboration from the student if necessary, until it becomes habit to keep talking for the entire allotted time.

Teaching Tips:

Remind the students to speak in present continuous when describing the image. ("The sun is shining. The man is looking at the woman as they walk across the beach. It looks like they are happy.")

If your student has a voice recorder or phone, have them record his/her responses. This will help track their progress as well as how long he/she speaks each time.

You can extend the activity into general speaking by having a discussion related to one or more of the photos.

Procedure:

1. In advance, prepare several photos for your student to describe to you.
2. Review some useful phrases (see examples above).
3. Show a photo to your student and ask him/her to describe it to you.
4. As needed, encourage your student to continue describing the photo.
5. Repeat if desired.

Test Prep: Reading Aloud Fluently

Time: 15 minutes

Level: Intermediate-Advanced

Materials Required: Prepared texts

Optional Materials: Recording device

Some standardized tests of English ability have a speaking task that evaluates how fluently the test taker can read a text aloud. To prepare your student for this, choose several short passages for him/her to read aloud. During class, first model reading the passage aloud and then have your student read it several times.

Give the student specific pointers after each reading. For example, if his/her intonation or stress needs improvement, mark the text to show which syllables to stress or where the intonation should rise or fall. If your student has a voice recorder or phone, have him/her record your reading as well as his/her final one for review and practice before your next lesson.

Teaching Tip:

I like to use *Breaking News English* for this activity because there are a number of activities for each story, so you can easily build an entire lesson around one or two passages.

Procedure:

1. In advance, prepare several short passages for your student to read aloud.
2. First, model reading the passage aloud, then have your student read it several times.
3. Monitor, and give specific pointers after each reading.
4. If your student has a voice recorder, have them record your reading as well as his/her final one for them to review and practice before your next lesson.

Test Prep Speaking Activity: 5Ws and H

Time: 30 minutes

Level: Intermediate-Advanced

Materials Required: Prepared speaking prompts, timer (phone, kitchen timer, etc.)

Optional Materials: Recording device

The speaking part of a standardized test of English ability has some similarities with the written essay portion: the test taker is asked to speak with minimal or no preparation time about a topic for a specified length of time. However, speaking tests have other elements as well. For example, some tests have speaking prompts focusing on personal experiences.

Some common prompts include:

Describe a person who has had a great influence on you.

What is your happiest childhood memory? Why?

Describe a place you like to visit.

To get full marks, test takers need to give a full answer. What "full answer" means varies among proficiency exams so do some research about what will be required of your student. However, a general tip is to have your student think like a journalist: 5Ws and H. To use the above example prompt of an influential person, your student should tell who the person is and how the person influenced him/her. Your student should elaborate by including when and where they met. He/she can emphasize how long they have known each other, why the person was influential, and what specific qualities the person has that impressed the student.

When you think your student is ready, provide a prompt and set the timer to give them one minute to prepare. When the timer goes off, reset the timer for two minutes and instruct the student to begin speaking. You may want to record the answers to track his/her progress.

Procedure:

1. In advance, prepare several speaking prompts for your student to answer.

2. You may want to have an example prompt to model fully answering a question.

3. Whether you model the activity or not, point out that the student will need to expand his/her answer to fill the time. Keeping the 5W and H questions in mind will help him/her remember to include a variety of details.

4. Give the student a prompt and set the timer for one minute to allow him/her to prepare a response.

5. When the timer goes off, reset it for two minutes and have the student begin speaking.

6. Your student can record their answers if they have a phone or voice recorder.

The "Expert" Conversation Activity

Time: 5-10 minutes

Level: Intermediate-Advanced

Materials Required: None

Both the teacher and student write down five things that they're an expert in. Once you've written your lists, circle the three that you would each like to talk about most.

After that, talk with the student about these topics that both of you have chosen for as long as the conversation is interesting or until the time you've allotted to this activity is up.

Teaching Tips:

This is a particularly useful activity for practicing many of the speaking sub-skills such as initiating a conversation, turn-taking, and appropriate length of responses. You can pre-teach some of these things before you begin the activity. For example, show your students how to initiate a conversation by saying something like, "I see you're interested in _____. What/where/why/when/who/how _____?"

Or you could teach your students about appropriate length of responses by doing one bad example and then one good example. Continue with the bad example by rambling on and on until the students are feeling a little bit uncomfortable and they'll see clearly what you mean.

Procedure:

1. Talk about what "expert" means with your student.

2. Both teach and student make a list of five items and then each choose the three things that you would most like to talk about.

3. Talk together for 5-6 minutes about the chosen topics. Make sure that starting the conversation, turn-taking and changing topics is partly up to the student and not just the teacher.

What Can I do with a _____?

Time: 5-10 minutes

Level: Beginner-Advanced

Materials Required: An object (something from your office or teacher's room)

Show your student some random common object (potatoes are often used for this activity, but I like to use some kind of "trash" to introduce a lesson on recycling.) Work together with the student to brainstorm as many possible uses for the item as possible. This is a fun way to get some creative juices flowing!

Procedure:

1. In advance, prepare an object. A potato is commonly used, but it can be anything.

2. Brainstorm creative uses for the object together.

Who do you Want at your Party?

Time: 5 minutes

Level: Intermediate-Advanced

Materials Required: None

This is an excellent activity for higher level students. Both you and your student can pick four famous people, dead or alive that you'd like to invite to a party you are having. Then, think about the reason why you're inviting them. I do an example like this:

Person: Barrack Obama

Reason: He seems like a fun guy to hang around with and maybe I can find out what it's really like to live in the White House.

Give your students a few minutes to prepare, depending on the level. Then, discuss your answers together.

Procedure:

1. Think about some famous people you'd want to invite to a party (the student does the same).

2. Give a few minutes of preparation time if required.

3. Discuss answers together.

Listening Focused Activities

Listening is a key skill that certainly deserves some focused attention in conversation or general English classes. Here are some of the best activities to consider trying out with your student.

20 Questions

Time: 5-15 minutes

Level: Beginner-Advanced

Materials Required: None

Listening for specific details is an important listening sub-skill. This game will help students practice that as they are required to listen carefully to each question and answer in order that they don't repeat one and waste a question.

This is a "20 questions" style game that can be based on any topic that you're teaching (animals, jobs, etc.) or you may want to leave it open to any person, place, or thing. It's ideal for helping students work on yes/no questions and answers as well as speaking and listening skills. It's vital that students listen to the other questions already asked in order to maximize their chance at guessing the secret thing.

The way it works is that one person thinks of a secret person, place, or thing and the other person asks up to 20 yes/no questions to try to find out what it is. Then, switch roles.

It's certainly possible to adapt this game to whatever unit you're teaching. For example, you could limit the secret thing to animals or jobs. In this case, I'll usually make it into a "10 questions" game because 20 is too easy in most cases.

Teaching Tips:

I use a few rules that make things go more smoothly:

1. A guess counts as a "question". This prevents random guesses which don't make the game very fun.

2. The person must use a full sentence to ask a question. The questions have to be yes/no type.

3. For children, emphasize that they must tell the truth at all times! Also, they should choose something that everyone knows, instead of some obscure, random thing.

Procedure:

1. Either the teacher or students chooses a secret person, place or thing. You may want to limit it to a certain area for beginners such as jobs or animals and also reduce the number of questions to 10.

2. The other person asks yes/no questions using complete sentences.

3. The game continues until the person has guessed the correct answer or has run out of questions. Switch roles and play another round or two.

Describing Something Guessing Game

Time: 5-10 minutes

Level: Beginner-Advanced

Materials Required: Handout or PowerPoint with approximately 20 pictures

Predicting content before hearing it is an important listening sub-skill for our students to practice. In this case, students take a look at the possibilities and can make some predictions about what they will hear. For example, if the person is a man or a woman. This also helps students work on listening for the key words in a statement.

This is a simple warm-up activity heavy on the listening that you can use to generate some interest in a topic. It can also be used as a quick review of the last lesson's contents. For beginners, it's best to play after you've taught them the necessary language to make the sentences instead of as a warm-up at the beginning of class.

Make up a handout or PowerPoint with pictures of around 20 famous people. It's helpful to do a brief parts of speech review for descriptive nouns and adjectives. Tell the student to listen specifically for these key words. Give some hints such as, "He is American," "He is a sport player," and, "He plays golf." As you can see, it helps the student work on the simple present tense.

By this time the student will have guessed Tiger Woods. Cross Tiger Woods off the list or remove it from the PowerPoint. Then, get the student to choose one person from the list and give you hints about him/her.

This activity works for almost any topic (animals/food/clothes, etc.) and is good for teenagers or adults.

Teaching Tips:

A speaking sub-skill that you could focus on using this activity is hedging, which is when we are not sure about something and use language to indicate that. For example, "Maybe it's _____," "It might be _____," "Is it _____?," "It could be _____. "

Or, you could have students practice the listening test skill of writing key words down as they listen. You should emphasize that students should not write the entire sentence they hear, only the descriptive nouns and adjectives, perhaps 1 word for each statement made.

I emphasize that students should speak in full sentences when they are giving hints to their partners. Simply saying things like, "Man, American, golf" is really not useful for helping students improve their English skills beyond the most basic beginners and even then it's questionable. It's useful to put some example sentences on the board such as: "She/He has _____ (hair/eyes).", "She/He is from _____.", and "She/He is a _____ (job)."

For real world contextualizing of listening try to provide relevant situations for students. One example might be when a student travels and meets a native English speaker who talks very quickly with an accent. Stress to students that listening is not a passive language act, and that they can actively ask follow-up questions in order to confirm what they've heard, or ask for more details. Some examples of follow-up questions might be: Is he African-

American? Is he rich? Does he do Nike ads? For beginners, questions like "Can you repeat that, please?" and "Could you speak more slowly, please?" are also extremely useful to practice and gain the confidence required to ask when they are unsure of what they've heard and are worried about 'losing face.' Feeling ashamed that their "English is poor" is a very prevalent attitude that most ESL/EFL speakers often say, especially in some countries.

As a general rule, the more that you can get your students speaking in full sentences, the better off they'll be in terms of language learning. It's far easier to let your students just say one or two words, but they're not actually pushing themselves to incorporate grammar constructions into their speech in a meaningful way. But, of course don't forget that spoken discourse has much shorter sentences than more formal written work, so don't push students to use more complicated grammatical constructions when doing a simple listening activity like this.

You can put in a few fun pictures to make it more interesting. For example, I'll always include a picture of myself in a situation where it might not look like me because I had a different hairstyle or was wearing glasses. Or, I'll put in a picture of my twin sister (I really do have a twin)!

Procedure:

1. Prepare pictures of famous people on a handout or in a PowerPoint slide.
2. Choose one person and give some hints describing them. The student tries to guess who it is.
3. Switch roles and continue until the time is up. In order to avoid frustration, I usually make a limit for each picture of two minutes because there might be one that the guesser really just doesn't know.

Dictation Practice

Time: 5-10 minutes

Level: Beginner-Advanced

Materials Required: A text to dictate

Dictation can help our students with some important listening sub-skills, including detecting transition signals (first, second, third, etc.), note taking, and listening for details. It also helps students practice a range of other things, from printing English letters to punctuation, spelling, proof-reading and lay-out. Dictation can also offer a serious dose of syntax, vocabulary and grammar! In short, it's an extremely versatile activity and a nice break from the very communicative activities that dominate most of our textbooks and classes today.

The way it works is that you find a writing passage that you'll read to your student. Or, you could even make up your own on the fly for a truly no-prep activity. In an emergency situation, just grab something off the shelf in your office or from your desk and it should work in most cases.

However, if you have a wee bit more time, some good sources for writing passages are the textbook you're using for the class, a website like *Breaking News English*, or just about anything for that matter! You may even want to write it yourself. The key is finding something at a similar level to your students, or just slightly below.

Read out the passage to your student who writes down what they hear. You may have to read it again, depending on the level. I generally give him/her a minute or two at the end for proofreading and instruct them to check things like spelling and punctuation. Check answers and correct any errors with spelling, punctuation, etc.

If you're teaching beginner level students, it may be a good idea to type out your dictation with single-word fill in the blanks in each sentence. You may even put two possible answers in parentheses after each blank. For example, "Jackie goes to _____ (the beach, the beats)." If you're feeling really motivated, and have the time and energy, you can also try making a dictation worksheet with words that only have prefixes and suffixes, and students must listen and complete the words. This is great for teaching spelling and you can help students learn how to listen/read parts of speech and their particular beginnings and endings; explain that if you know how different parts of speech are spelled, for example verbs often end with -ing, then you can more easily write down what you're listening to, and on tests you can guess the meaning of a word more effectively if you know what part of speech it might belong to.

For intermediate and advanced students, it's important to help them learn skills like anticipating what comes next in the dictation. Teach and review briefly things like collocations (high frequency groupings of words) that students can use to reduce stress and anxiety when listening. Give an example like, "How are _____ _____? (you today). Tell students to think about the context of the listening dictation, and that context + collocations can often help them fill in words they might have missed writing down.

Also, an easy and fast way to find listening strategies to teach students is to consider what you would do if you were a student in your own class and break these down into micro-skills and strategies. If you really want to challenge students, paraphrasing or summarizing the dictation passage are incredibly useful skills that are often weak or unpracticed. Ask students to write, for example, a summary of the dictation passage in one sentence that has the main idea and maybe a few key details. Be sure that you have a summary sentence of your own to show students as an ideal example if you do this.

Procedure:

1. Choose a passage that you'll read to your student.

2. Read the passage and the student writes down what they hear.

3. Give some time for proofreading and editing at the end.

4. Check their work.

Dictogloss

Time: 10-15 minutes

Level: Intermediate-Advanced

Materials Required: A short story

This is a simple activity for higher level students that helps them practice their listening and memory skills, as well as substituting vocabulary words if the original word is no longer accessible to them. It's also heavy on the sub-skill of listening for gist, as students have to distinguish the main ideas of what they hear from the supporting ideas. Plus, they'll have to take some notes about the main ideas. Remind them that this is a useful skill for listening tests that have long passages they have to remember details from in order to choose the correct answers.

There are some common discourse markers that are used to signal transitions in a story or conversation. Tell students to listen for transition signals in order to focus on key info. "After that, I ACTION." ". . . because of X, I then did ACTION."

The teacher might also tell students to write down the elements of a story structure beside which to write in point form the key words: setting/place, who/actors, rising action, climax, falling action, and resolution/outcome/denouement. For advanced students, a brief review of story genre features also helps them to anticipate the structure of the story and what and where they need to focus their listening.

You can find a short, interesting story of some kind or make up one yourself. I've used various things from children's stories to a story about something I did on the weekend. Just about anything can work.

Tell the story 1-3 times, depending on the student level and of course you can also vary your speaking speed to make this activity easier or harder. The student has to try to recreate what they heard. Emphasize that they won't be able to recreate the exact story that you told, but that they should try their best to keep the meaning the same. Then, they compare what they have with the original version.

This activity works well as a writing activity too instead of speaking.

Teaching Tips:

If you use something "scandalous," it will make the activity a lot more fun! Of course, it should still be appropriate so just picture your boss observing your class to decide if you should use it or not.

Procedure:

1. Prepare a short story which you'll read to your student.

2. Read the story the first time.

3. The student tries to remember the details of the story and can take some notes about it.

4. Read the story again and the student attempts to recreate the story more closely.

5. Do the previous step another time if required.

6. The student says (or writes) their final story and then compares with the original

Excuse Me, What did You Say?

Time: 10-15 minutes

Level: Intermediate-Advanced

Materials Required: Listening passage

It's often the case that we have to infer meaning from something, even though we didn't understand 100% of the words spoken. It may be a noisy restaurant or bar, the person is speaking very quietly, or for any other reason. This activity helps our students out with this skill.

Tell the student that you're going to read something to them but that you've been teaching all day and your voice is tired or weak. Or, use a different accent or speak very quickly. Whatever the case, make sure that not all the words can be understood easily. The student can jot down some notes as this is happening with key words.

After reading the passage, he/she has to try to figure out the main ideas even though they didn't understand everything. You may also allow the student to ask some clarification questions.

Procedure:

1. Choose a listening passage to read out loud.

2. Read it in a way that's a little bit difficult to understand (too fast, tired or weak voice, etc.).

3. The student jots down the key words they hear and thinks about the main ideas.

4. Discuss these ideas together with the student.

5. Read the passage again in a more easily understood voice.

Find the Details

Time: 5-10 minutes

Level: Beginner-Advanced

Materials Required: Listening passage

Listening for specific information is a key skill for our students to practice. In real life, they may have to see if a certain announcement at an airport is for their flight or a different one. For English proficiency exams, they may have to listen to a passage to find answers to very specific questions that they read ahead of time.

Something we can do to help our student out with this is to practice this in class! Find a listening passage and then ask the student to listen for very specific bits of information. For example, it could be something related to bus schedules and departure times. They might have to find out:

- When bus 1034 is leaving tonight

- Where bus 3221 is going to

- If bus 422 is full or not

- Etc.

Of course, tailor the listening passage and specific information to look for to the needs of your student. If he/she is preparing for a TOEFL listening test or wants to travel to the USA confidently, then this kind of activity will look very different.

Procedure:

1. Find an appropriate listening passage.

2. Tell the student to listen for some specific piece of information.

3. Check answers together.

Main Ideas Only Please!

Time: 5-10 minutes

Level: Intermediate-Advanced

Materials Required: Listening passage

This is a simple listening activity that helps students work on the important sub-skills of distinguishing the main ideas from the supporting details, along with note taking.

Find a listening passage at the appropriate level. I find that someone telling a story of some kind often works better than a conversation for this activity. Tell the student that they'll have to summarize what they heard in only 1-2 sentences and that they should just jot down a few key words for notes. Emphasize that they are NOT to repeat word for word what they hear, but they'll have to summarize instead.

Let the student listen once and take some notes. Then, play it again and the student can gather some more information. After that, give him/her some time to finalize their 1-2 sentence summary to read out loud to you. The teacher and student can discuss it together.

Procedure:

1. Choose an appropriate listening passage.

2. Tell the student that they will have to summarize it at the end and to write down only the key words.

3. Play it the first time. The student jots down a few key words.

4. Play it a second time. The student gather more information.

5. The student makes a 1-2 sentence summary of what they heard.

6. Discuss the answer together.

Secret Person

Time: 10-20 minutes

Level: Beginner-Intermediate

Materials Required: None

This is the perfect activity for using "be" statements in the past tense. Each of you can think of two dead people and write down their details: when they were born, where they were from, why they were famous, how they died, and one or two more interesting things.

To focus on careful listening, I usually will only repeat each clue once. Take turns giving clues to each other and then making guesses about who the people are. Ask some follow-up questions if the clues didn't give it away.

Procedure:

1. The teacher and the student each choose two dead people and write some hints about him/her. Giving around 5-6 hints is best. Be sure to start with the hardest ones and get to the easiest ones at the end.

2. Give hints to each other to try to figure out the secret people.

3. Ask some follow-up questions if necessary.

Reading Focused Activities

Students who are preparing for English proficiency exams or studying abroad for example will probably want to improve their reading skills. Here are lots of engaging, student-centred activities that you might want to try out.

Activate Prior Knowledge

Time: 5 minutes

Level: Beginner-Advanced

Materials Required: None

One of the most helpful things we can do for our students before they read something is to help activate their prior knowledge and set the context. An excellent way to do this for our student is to get them to talk about something before reading.

For example, maybe the text is a story about a vacation gone wrong. You can elicit some answers from the student about bad things that can happen on vacation and add some of your own as well. For example:

- Getting robbed

- Missing a flight

- Losing a wallet or passport

- Getting sick

- Etc.

Then, talk with the student for a couple of minutes about if any of these things have happened to them. This helps them activate any prior knowledge they may have about vocabulary they could expect to read, as well as to personalize it. Both of these things will make for a richer, more valuable reading experience and can help bring some real life into the classroom.

This activity can easily lead into other reading exercises and activities.

Agony Aunt

Time: 15-20 minutes

Level: Intermediate-Advanced

Materials Required: Printed advice column questions and answers

This activity will get your student talking because everyone knows how to solve other people's problems! If your student is a bit more advanced, you can use actual advice columns. These can easily be found by searching on the Internet for "advice column" etc. The lower the level, the more you'll need to grade the language or you can write your own advice column.

In terms of reading sub-skills, I like to get my students to take some notes as they're reading in order to work on their note-taking skills. It also helps with reading for detail and inferring the attitude or feeling of the person writing the letter.

I've done several variations of this activity and it has always been a hit. I begin with an introduction that shows a few advice column letters and answers. Discuss them a bit—most students will be familiar with the concept. Then, give your student a copy of a letter (not the same one from the introduction) and they'll need to read it and think of some advice. This could also be quite a nice homework assignment if you've just taught about should/shouldn't.

Teaching Tip:

If you are familiar with local celebrities popular with your student, you can use current gossip to spice up the lesson. If X pop star has just had a public breakup, write a letter from that person asking for help getting back together, finding a new boyfriend, etc.

Procedure:

1. Show some level-appropriate advice column letters. Read them together and discuss.

2. Give the student one more advice column together. They read it and then offer some advice.

3. Discuss the advice together.

An Irrelevant Sentence

Time: 5-20 minutes

Level: Beginner-Advanced

Materials Required: Texts with one irrelevant sentence

A key reading sub-skill is the ability to understand the text type and organization of it. For example, an email clearly has a different organizational style than a novel would. This activity is designed to help students recognize things that seem out of place when considering the text type. This requires both reading for detail and recognizing links between parts of a text.

The way it works is that the teacher prepares one, or more than one reading texts, inserting an irrelevant sentence into each one. How obvious to make it depends on the level of the students. The student has to use their reading for details skills to find which sentence doesn't belong.

Procedure:

1. Prepare some reading texts with one irrelevant sentence in each one.

2. The student reads each one and chooses the rogue sentence.

3. Discuss why it doesn't fit.

Brochure Scanning

Time: 10-20 minutes

Level: Beginner-Advanced

Materials Required: Travel brochures (scan and send the file to the student)

Scanning is reading for specific information and it makes an excellent ESL reading activity. Language learners tend to focus on trying to understand every word, so they need to practice quickly finding specific key words. This will increase their reading speed in general and help move them towards more natural reading practices.

To provide realistic practice, collect travel brochures, bus timetables and menus. If you do not have local access to any of these, a quick Google search will give you a wide variety. Here are a few sample scenarios to use, depending on the level of your student.

Option #1: Intermediate-Advanced Student

Find a vacation bargain. Give the student a budget, length of travel, and any other limitations, such as "type" of holiday (beach, historical, adventure, etc.). This is highly variable according to the materials you have available and student levels.

The student should scan the brochure for trips that match the criteria. To add more speaking, begin by discussing the students' ideas of a great vacation, and then work together to find a trip that matches those criteria.

Option #2: High Beginner Student

Try a new restaurant. Have the student find menu items with certain qualities, such as vegetarian, lamb, or no onions. Can he/she make a reservation for 8PM on Monday? What is the phone number for reservations? And so on.

Option #3: Beginner Student

Take a bus from point A to point B for a meeting at a given time and then return. Have the student use a bus timetable to plan the journey. Have him/her quickly scan the brochure to find the requested information.

Teaching Tips:

For lower level students, have printed questions for them to use with the brochure. For example, "What time is the last bus to _____ on Sunday nights?"

If you are looking online for printable realia, add "PDF" to your search and the results will begin with PDF files that match your search terms.

Or, if you can get a Flight Centre or Thomson brochure, you can get a lot of mileage out of it beyond scanning. They are basically magazines with hundreds of travel packages of all types and for a range of budgets, although nothing is too luxurious. The higher the level of the student, the more freedom you have to expand the activity.

Procedure:

1. In advance, get a brochure and scan it or find one on the Internet. Restaurant menus, bus timetables and travel brochures are perfect for this. See the examples above for some ideas.

2. Prepare some questions for the student to answer using the information in the brochure.

3. Explain to the student that they are not to read word for word. They should only be reading to find the answers to the questions.

4. Have him/her find answers to the questions and check them together.

Chapter Response

Time: 10-15 minutes

Level: Intermediate-Advanced

Materials Required: None

Optional Materials: Printed list of questions

Chapter endings make handy stopping points to check your student's comprehension and build a bit of interest to keep up motivation for the next chapter. These questions can be answered orally as part of a book discussion or written in a reader response journal and then discussed in class.

Some questions you can ask include:

What surprised you in this chapter?

What feelings did you have as you read? What made you feel this way?

What words, phrases, or situations in the chapter would you like to have explained?

Would you recommend this novel to someone else? Why or why not?

How do the events in this story so far relate to your life?

Which character do you most relate to? In what way?

Which character most reminds you of someone in your life? In what way?

What do you hope to learn about (a character) as you continue reading?

What do you think will happen next?

What questions do you have that you hope will be answered in the next chapter?

I also like to include some questions related to discourse markers and how the text is organized. This can really help our students gain an awareness of the key differences among kinds of texts that they read. Finally, I also try to ask some very leading questions about links between various parts of the texts and how they connect to each other.

Procedure:

1. In advance, prepare a printed list of questions about the chapter.

2. Discuss together or have the student write their answers for homework and you can discuss them in the next class.

Character Problems and Solutions

Time: 10-15 minutes

Level: Intermediate-Advanced

Materials Required: None

This is a post-reading activity to include in a novel study or use with a short story. Choose a problem a character faced in the story. Discuss the problem and how the character solved it. Then, have your students brainstorm other ways the problem could have been dealt with. This is a sneaky grammar lesson. You can teach modals of regret (could/should/would have done/etc.) without getting too personal with your students.

In terms of reading sub-skills, it's heavy on inferring attitude, feelings and meaning. I also like to get my students to predict what could happen next if the text is unclear about it.

Procedure:

1. Choose a problem a character faced in the story.

2. Discuss the problem and how the character solved it.

3. Have your student brainstorm other ways the problem could have been dealt with.

Closest in Meaning

Time: 10 minutes

Level: Intermediate-Advanced

Materials Required: Sentences with corresponding match options

It's often the case when reading anything in a language that we're not fluent in to encounter words we don't know. Some people reach for their dictionary every single time this happens but this isn't necessary and it's certainly not efficient. Instead, a more effective way is to guess the meaning of the unknown word using context clues. This activity is designed to help our students with this important skill.

Make some sentences and for each one, have 2-3 corresponding sentences, one of which is obviously closest in meaning to the original than the other ones. I use a slightly higher level of vocabulary than the student is at and don't allow them to use their dictionaries. For example:

Focus: The professor delivered her lecture eloquently.

Answer: The professor's lesson was clear and easy to understand.

Extra Sentence 1: The professor's lecture was presented in a PowerPoint.

Extra Sentence 2: The professor's class was spoken too quickly.

Procedure:

1. In advance, write some sentences and some corresponding sentences. One should be closer in meaning to the original than the others and use some higher-level vocabulary throughout.

2. The student has to choose the sentence that is closest in meaning to the original using context clues.

3. Check answers with the student and discuss helpful context clues used in the activity.

Disappearing Words

Time: 5 minutes

Level: Beginner-Intermediate

Materials Required: Whiteboard

This vocabulary game is an easy way to force students to keep a set of new vocabulary words in their heads, or to review past words. Write down 10-15 words on the whiteboard and give the student 1-2 minutes to study them.

Then, ask your student to close their eyes as you choose one or two words to erase. The student opens their eyes and has to tell you what is missing and where it was. You can either write those words in their spots again or add new words to the mix and continue the game.

Procedure:

1. Write down 10-15 vocabulary words on the whiteboard.

2. Have the student close their eyes as you erase 1-2 words.

3. The student opens their eyes and tells you which words are missing and where they were.

4. You can write those same words back in, or add new words to the mix in those same spots and continue the game.

Extensive Reading

Time: Variable

Level: Intermediate-Advanced

Materials Required: Graded readers or novels

It's often the case that students have to read for detail, but reading just for fun in

English is not something that they often do. That's why I like to include some extensive reading in my classes whenever it's practical. For online teaching, this is best done as a homework activity outside of class.

The key is that students choose something to read that's slightly before their level. Then, they can just read it easily without having to worry about stopping every minute or two to look up a word. I emphasize to my students that the goal is to work on reading fluency and to put away their dictionary and just read for fun. This will usually require some help from the teacher with regards to reading material choices.

Procedure:

1. The student choose something to read at a level slightly below where they're at, with some help from the teacher.

2. Read for 10-15 minutes a day outside of class.

3. Briefly discuss how the reading is going with the student in class.

Find the Reference

Time: 10+ minutes

Level: Beginner-Intermediate

Materials Required: Newspaper article, pen

This is a noticing activity that helps students recognize links within a text. In newspaper writing, care is taken to avoid repetitive use of the subject's name. This is the opposite of most ESL material, which makes frequent use of repetition to reinforce language. Your student will read a newspaper article and circle all references to the subject in order to practice recognizing the subject even when various terms are used to reference it. For a completed example of this activity, please see: *www.eslspeaking.org/reference.*

Teaching Tip:

Use an actual newspaper, rather than a source such as *Breaking News English*, which may alter the text to reduce the use of varied referents.

Procedure:

1. Choose an article from a newspaper that has multiple references to the subject but uses a number of different referents such as, "Jones," "he," "him," "the 39-year-old," "the painter," "the father of two," etc.

2. Have the student read and circle each reference to the subject.

3. Check answers together.

Flyer Time

Time: 10+ minutes

Level: Beginner-Intermediate

Materials Required: Prepared flyers/ads and questions

This activity is used to practice answering questions with a visual aid. This activity is designed to assist students with predicting and then scanning for specific information as well as inferring meaning from the context if the answer is not explicitly stated.

While your student is unlikely to be asked which bands are playing at X festival, they may need to answer questions about a presentation or report in English. In advance, prepare several event flyers or ads and questions. Prepare some questions that have the answers clearly stated:

"What time will _____ begin?"

"Where will this take place?"

Also include some questions that require the student to think about the event and use existing knowledge:

"Who do you think will be attending this event?"

"Will attendees need to do anything in advance?" (For example, make a reservation or buy tickets)

Give your student access to a scanned version of the flyer and get them to answer the questions. Explain that not all of the answers are stated explicitly.

Procedure:

1. In advance, prepare several event flyers and questions (see above for examples) for your students to answer using the flyers. Scan and send them to the student.

2. Let your student know that not all questions are explicitly answered on the flyer.

3. Have your studens use the flyer to answer the questions.

4. Ask the questions. Do not let your student read the answers word for word.

Headline Prediction Practice

Time: 5-10 minutes

Level: Intermediate-Advanced

Materials Required: Text with a headline

One way to improve reading skills is to have in mind what we're about to read. This primes our brains to receive information and by doing this, reading comprehension is generally better. It's also helpful to have some key vocabulary words in mind. Furthermore, do a modeling of asking the 5Ws + H (who, what, where, when, why and how) about key words in a sample title with intermediate students, and with advanced (depending on the class) give a brief reminder to use those questions when predicting

To do this with your student, choose a story that has an interesting headline that is somewhat vague and could have many possible outcomes or reasons. Elicit some answers from the student but don't give away too much! Write on the whiteboard or in a PPT slide 3-4 different ideas that the student has.

Give access to the text for the student to read and they can quickly read through it to see which of their predictions was correct, if any. This can lead into a more detailed second reading activity.

Procedure:

1. Show the student an interesting headline.

2. The student can predict what might happen, or what the cause of the problem is.

3. Elicit some answers and write 3-4 of them on the board.

4. The student quickly reads the text to see if any of their guesses were correct.

Identify This!

Time: 5-10 minutes

Level: Beginner

Materials Required: A text

Beginners are often at the level where they are just beginning to understand the vocabulary words and basic grammatical constructions within a text. This activity can help them with this.

The way it works is that you can choose a certain thing that the student has to look for within a reading passage. It may be as simple as finding all the numbers, colors, weather words, etc. Or, the student may have to find verbs in the past tense. I generally choose this based on what I've been teaching my student in the past few lessons.

Procedure:

1. Choose a text with various examples of your target grammar or vocabulary.

2. Explain to the student what they should be looking for (past tense verbs for example) and that they should circle each example they find.

3. Check answers.

4. This activity can easily lead into other reading exercises with the same text. Or, it could be a post-reading activity as well.

Paraphrasing and Summarizing Practice

Time: Variable

Level: Intermediate-Advanced

Materials Required: Passage to paraphrase (lecture, newspaper article, etc.)

Paraphrasing and summarizing are important writing skills and there is certainly some overlap between the two. If your student is planning to take a test such as the TOEFL, TOEIC, or IELTS, they will need to be able to do these things effectively. What's the difference? Paraphrasing is expressing the meaning of something using different words with the goal to achieve greater clarity and includes some degree of analysis. Summarizing is giving an overview of the main points of something.

To help your student practice paraphrasing, choose a short newspaper article. He/she can begin by circling words which cannot be changed: places, names, dates, etc. Then, see if any information can be combined or rearranged. Next, consider the best synonyms to replace the nouns, verbs, and adjectives. Finally, reread the original text and compare it with the paraphrase. Do both texts have the same meaning? If not, keep trying.

Many students think that summarizing a text is extremely difficult but it's possible to work on this skill with them. You may want to do a warm-up exercise by choosing a popular movie that students have seen. Ask them to summarize the story in one sentence. If you're working with intermediate students, consider putting a fill in the blank summary sentence on the board to help them. Once they realize they already do summaries in their day to day lives, they'll have more confidence that they can do the 'academic' style too.

Teaching Tip:

For advanced students, it may be possible to have them do both summarizing and paraphrasing together. However, for intermediate students it's important to only ask them to do one of the two, and later if they've mastered each, try doing both of them in the same activity.

Procedure for Paraphrasing:

1. Give the student a passage that they can read.

2. The student decides which words can't be changed and are most important.

3. The student decides which information can be combined or rearranged, as well as think of some alternative synonyms to use.

4. He/she prepares their final paraphrase draft and the teacher can check it.

Procedure for Summarizing:

1. Choose a movie or something that the student is familiar with that has a story element to it.

2. Ask him/her to summarize the story in one sentence

3. Check the sentence.

Proofreading Practice

Time: 5-10 minutes

Level: Beginner-Advanced

Materials Required: Worksheet with errors

The ability to correct errors through proofreading and editing is a very important reading and writing skill. However, there's more to it than just telling our students to find the mistakes! We can actually teach them how to do this in a far more systematic way.

How you design this activity will vary greatly depending on the level of your students. Beginner level students can generally only proofread 1-3 things when they start developing self-editing skills. For example, tell them to check that the first word of each sentence is capitalized and has a period at the end. Advanced level students can handle a wide range of errors that include punctuation, spelling, grammar, vocabulary, flawed logic and more.

Not proofreading writing is the biggest writing mistake. This applies to students who are studying English as a second or third language, as well as native speakers. Here's the advice that I give my students about this important topic.

After you write, allow yourself some time to read your work. If you're doing a writing test that is one hour long, I recommend the following:

1. 5 minutes planning. Write a few notes. Make a plan. What is your first, second, and third main point (if writing an essay)?

2. 45-50 minutes writing.

3. 5-10 minutes proofreading. Check writing for any mistakes. I recommend double-spacing, so it's easy to make any changes if you need to. Cross off what you wrote and then write in the line above it.

Reading out loud each and every word is a good habit to get into. Pay close attention to things like subject-verb agreement (He is, She goes), spelling, capital letters, punctuation, etc.

If students do only one thing to improve their writing, it's this! ALWAYS proofread. Always! Here's a proofreading checklist I made for my university students in South Korea but it may be a bit too academically focused for your teaching context: *www.jackiebolen.com/proofreading.*

Procedure:

1. Explain to your student about proofreading and give them a checklist for things to check.

2. Prepare a worksheet of sentences, a paragraph or an essay (depending on the level) that has some errors from the checklist on it.

3. The student has to go through the worksheet finding the errors. Check answers together.

Puzzles

Time: Homework activity

Level: Beginner-Intermediate

Materials Required: A puzzle

Puzzles are an excellent way to review vocabulary and I find that most students enjoy doing them, particularly teenagers. They help students read for detail as they have to pay close attention to exactly what the clue says in order to answer the question correctly. For online teaching, it's best done as a homework activity.

It's really easy to make puzzles yourself using something like *Discovery.com*'s Puzzlemaker (*www.discoveryeducation.com/free-puzzlemaker*) and it's actually the preferable option since you can include all the specific vocabulary that you'd like. I prefer to use the criss-cross option because it has the most educational benefit since it deals with meanings as well as vocabulary words.

Procedure:

1. Go to *Discovery.com* and find the Puzzlemaker.

2. Design your puzzle (criss-cross is best!), using words and definitions. Alternatively, you could give hints about the word related to the context you'd use it in instead of the actual definition. Here are two examples:

   ○ This animal has black and white stripes (skunk).

   ○ If a _____ sprays you, you'll smell really bad (skunk).

3. Have the student complete the puzzle for homework.

Same Same but Different

Time: 5-10 minutes

Level: Beginner-Advanced

Materials Required: Text

This is a simple reading activity that requires students to identify the key points of a text and to also work on note taking. In advance, prepare two slightly different versions of a text with a few key things changed.

The student reads the first version and takes notes. Then, they read another version that has some changes (the amount depends on the length of the passage and level of students) but I usually tell my student how many changes I've made before the second reading. The student can take notes about the changes. Of course, the student should put away the first version where they won't be tempted to look at it! Instead, he/she has to rely on their notes and their memory.

Procedure:

1. Choose a text.

2. The student reads the passage and takes notes about the key points. Put away the original paper.

3. Tell the student that they're going to read a slightly different version with some key things that are changed. Let him/her know how many changes there are.

4. The student reads the new version and compares the changes from the original.

5. Check answers together.

Scanning

Time: 5 minutes

Level: Beginner-Advanced

Materials Required: A text

Scanning means to read a text quickly while searching for specific information or facts. This is necessary to do in a number of real life situations, not to mention for English reading proficiency tests. However, without some targeted activities and practice, most students don't naturally do this in another language!

One way to help our student with scanning is to find a short text and then prepare some simple true/false questions. Show the questions to the student first and then give him/her only a short amount of reading time to find the answers.

It is important to stress that he/she should identify—and circle or underline the specific information that will answer the questions so that they don't read every word and practice the skill of scanning—this is especially important for beginner (doing a brief demonstration is also a good idea) and low intermediate students, and even sometimes for advanced too.

At the end of the reading time, the student turns their papers over and tries to answer the questions. This scanning activity can lead into a more detailed second reading exercise.

Procedure:

1. Talk about scanning and why it's an important reading skill.

2. Give the student some simple true/false questions related to a text.

3. Allow a short amount of time for reading.

4. The student answers the questions.

5. Check answers together.

Skimming

Time: 5 minutes

Level: Intermediate-Advanced

Materials Required: A text

Skimming means to read quickly in order to get a general overview of the information. It's vital that our students are able to do this because we're required to do this in many real-life situations (as well as for academic purposes). For example, it's not common to read a travel brochure word-for-word. Instead, we quickly look through it to get a general idea of what it says in order to make a decision.

One way to help our student do this is to limit how long they can take to do a first quick read-through of a text. First, give the student some very basic comprehension questions that aim at the big picture of the text. Allow him/her some time to read them. Then, give the student a very short amount of time for skimming. At the end of the allotted time, the student turns the text over and attempts to answer the questions. Then check answers together.

Teaching Tip:

Absolute beginners who are trying to understand a text word by word will not be able to do this activity effectively so I recommend it only for high-beginners and above. In addition, there is a large variance between what this activity will look like for a high-beginner student and one who is advanced. More advanced students will be able to handle longer and more complicated texts, more difficult questions and a greater number of them.

Procedure:

1. Talk about skimming, why it's necessary and how to do it.

2. Give the student some comprehension questions related to a text.

3. Allow the student a very short amount of reading time.

4. Check answers together.

Story Timeline

Time: 10-15 minutes

Level: Beginner-Advanced

Materials Required: Sentence strips of important events in a novel

Extensive reading is an excellent way to build your students' vocabulary quickly, but you and your student probably don't want to spend too much class time reading novels. One option is to assign a novel for homework and in each lesson, go over unfamiliar vocabulary or situations as well as any number of extension activities.

In terms of reading sub-skills, an activity like this one can be very useful for a number of reasons. It helps students gain a greater understanding of discourse markers, links between sections of the text and also an awareness of the type of text they're reading.

A timeline, or chronology, of important plot events is a useful way to have the class briefly summarize the story chapter by chapter. A timeline will help them keep track of the story while providing practice determining important events.

To do this, prepare some strips of paper with the main events of the novel or reading passage. The student has to put them in the correct order.

Teaching Tips:

For higher-level students, consider adding extra, unimportant plot events and have the students select only the important ones to order.

Penguin has six levels of graded readers that include simplified versions of popular novels and classics that you may want to consider using with your students.

Procedure:

1. In advance, prepare sentence strips describing important events in the plot.
2. Have the student order the sentence strips you have provided.

Think about the Characters More Deeply

Time: 15+ minutes

Level: Intermediate-Advanced

Materials Required: Fiction reading

When reading fiction, here are some ideas to help students think about the characters more deeply which will help them understand the overall text.

- Make a fact file about the main character. Here are some things to include in this section. How old is the character? Who is in their family? What is their job?

- Compare and contrast two main characters in the story. How are they the same? How are they different?

- Usually, the main character in a story changes in some way by the end. How did the main character in the story you have just read change in their actions or thinking? How were they at the beginning? What was different at the end? What caused them to change?

- Consider one scene from a different character's point of view. In English, we say every fight has three sides: your version, my version, and the truth. This is because all of us see the same event in different ways.

- Think of a situation that is not in the book. What would the main character do in that situation? Why do you think so?

Think about the Plot More Carefully

Time: 15+ minutes

Level: Intermediate-Advanced

Materials Required: Fiction reading

If you teach novels or short stories in your classes, then you could consider doing this activity. Thinking about the plot more carefully will also improve your reading comprehension skills. Here are some ideas to help our students consider the storyline more deeply.

- Make a timeline of important events in the story. How does one event lead to another?

- Where does the action occur? Make a list of important locations in the story. Would the story be the same in any location? Why or why not?

- When you read a book in English, write a review on *Goodreads* or *Amazon*. Let the world know what you thought of the book.

- Make a summary of what you read in 3-4 sentences (either writing or speaking out loud to yourself).

- Pretend you are the character in the story. Write a postcard from a certain point in time to another character.

- Draw a map of the book's setting.

- Create a poem about a book or story character.

- Write a diary entry as if you were a person in the story.

Use Context Clues

Time: 10+ minutes

Level: Intermediate-Advanced

Materials Required: Story or novel

This activity helps students develop their ability to use context clues when reading. Simply have them write down five words they do not know as they are reading. Have them note the page number and paragraph for easy reference. Once they have finished reading, have them find those words again and write down the sentence it is used in as well as the sentence before and after it.

Instruct the student to note if there is a prefix or suffix, and what part of speech the unknown word might belong to. Next, write down the word that is before the unknown word, and the word after it. Ask them if those help to infer the meaning of the unknown word. After that, write down 2-3 words before, and 2-3 words after, the unknown word (if there are any) to see if those help. Lastly, write down the sentence before, and the sentence after, the unknown word sentence.

Once they have written these sentences, have them use the sentences to guess the meaning of each unknown word and write that as well. Finally, have them compare their guess to the dictionary definition. Are they close? If not, was the word used in an ambiguous way, or could they have made better use of context clues?

Teaching Tip:

Once the student is familiar with this activity, consider relegating it to homework.

Procedure:

1. As an addition to a regular reading activity, have your student make note of five words in the story they do not know and make note of each word, the page number, and the paragraph number and continue reading.

2. Once he/she has finished reading, go back and find those words again and write down the sentence it is used in as well the sentence before and after it.

3. Then, have your student use the sentences to guess the meaning of each unknown word and write that as well.

4. Have the student compare their guesses with the dictionary definitions of each word.

What are you Watching Tonight?

Time: 10-15 minutes

Level: Intermediate-Advanced

Materials Required: TV guide

Maybe you've had a student complain that what they have to read in ESL/EFL textbooks is too boring! If this is the case, mix it up a little bit and bring some real life into the classroom. Take a look online for a TV schedule or guide and send a copy to your student.

Then, ask him/her some questions such as what show is playing at a certain time. Or, to choose a show they want to watch at 7pm tonight and tell you why. These kinds of questions help the student work on their scanning skills as they have to look quickly for very specific information.

Finally, the student can take a turn asking you some questions. This quick activity can certainly lead into a full lesson on TV, hobbies, TV stars, etc.

Procedure:

1. Find a TV guide online and send one copy to your student.

2. Ask the student some questions based on it.

3. The student can ask you some questions too.

What's the Main Idea?

Time: 10-20 minutes (depends on the length of the text)

Level: Intermediate-Advanced

Materials Required: A text

An important reading sub-skill is the ability to pick out the key points and summarize.

This is important in real life for things like reading reports or preparing for a test, but also for English reading proficiency exams. This simple activity is designed to practice this skill.

Give the student a text appropriate to their level. More advanced students can handle longer ones. Ask the student to read through it carefully, taking notes as they do this about the main points. Or, they may wish to circle or highlight key words.

Then, the student has to summarize the main idea of the article in 1-3 sentences. How many sentences depends on the length of the text. Discuss the answers together.

I generally have an "ideal" summary for the student to compare theirs to but of course, there are many different versions possible. The main thing is that student is able to communicate the main idea or points of the text. However, by showing a summary it's possible to set a standard for testing and grading that the student can use to compare their own to and get an idea of what they need to practice and improve upon.

Procedure:

1. Choose an appropriate text.

2. The student reads the text, taking notes or circling key words.

3. He/she summarizes it in 1-3 sentences

4. Discuss it together with the student.

Writing Focused Activities

Out of all the skills, writing is often the one that I get students to work on for homework. After all, most parents or students themselves don't want to pay you to "teach" them for 30 minutes if they're writing something by themselves for 20 minutes of it!

In this section, there are a few quick writing activities that can be done in class and then also some ideas for homework assignments.

5 Senses

Time: 5 minutes

Level: Intermediate-Advanced

Materials Required: An object

This activity is a fun way to help students work on descriptive writing. Ask your student to bring an everyday food item to class with them like a carrot or kind of drink. It should be something that you can eat or drink in order to do the "taste" sense. The student has to write down a few descriptive words for each sense (see, smell, feel, hear, taste). Obviously, "hear" will not be easy for a carrot, but you could tell your student to think about what happens when you snap a carrot in half.

When the time is up, talk about what the student has written down. You can also do this activity with another object if you wish. It works well as a daily warm-up in a writing class, if you use a different object each day. It's also possible to do this as a speaking activity.

Procedure:

1. Get the student to bring an object to class that you can eat or drink.

2. He/she has to think of a few words for each of the senses related to that object (see, smell, feel, hear, taste) and write them down.

3. At the end of the allotted time, talk together about what the student wrote down and add some of your own words.

4. Do another round with a different object if you'd like. Or, make it a regular warmer activity.

ABC Order

Time: 5 minutes

Level: Beginner

Materials Required: Worksheet/whiteboard

Young students and those whose first languages do not use the Latin alphabet need to practice alphabetic order. Have your student order the vocabulary alphabetically. For the lowest level beginners, have no more than one word starting with any given letter.

Procedure:

1. In advance, prepare several vocabulary words on a worksheet, depending on the age and level of the student.

2. With young students, begin with the Alphabet Song.

3. Then, the student can put several words in alphabetical order, with or without your help depending on the level.

Association

Time: 10-20 minutes

Level: Intermediate-Advanced

Materials Required: List of words related to a theme

A fun way to get students writing is this "association game." Think of a number of words related to a certain theme. For example, the theme of travel could use the following words: holidays, relax, vacation, transportation, food, etc.

You can say these words one by one and the student has to write down the first word that comes to mind when you say it. Using the list from above, they might write: Thailand, beach, fun, motorcycle, curry.

When this is done, the student can write a story using the words they've thought of. It may or may not be a true story, but it doesn't really matter either way. This makes an excellent homework activity for online teaching. To make it more fun, I require that the student must use every word they wrote down once! This leads to some interesting plot twists. Of course, remind your student to spend some time proofreading and editing before sharing the story with you in the next class.

Procedure:

1. Think of at least 5-10 words related to a certain theme or topic.

2. Say the words one by one and the student has to write down the first word that comes to mind.

3. Using these words, the student has to write a story. It can be true or not true.

4. Read through it together in the next class.

Boggle

Time: 10 minutes

Level: Intermediate-Advanced

Materials Required: Boggle board

You've probably played the word game Boggle before. You shake up the letters and then have a certain amount of time to make some words with connecting letters. It's possible to play it with students but you don't need the actual Boggle game.

Make up a grid on the whiteboard, PowerPoint or on a piece of paper. It only takes a minute to do this. I make a 6x6 grid and randomly write letters in the squares. Just make sure that students can see it well. Then, make as many words as possible that are 4+ letters. You can play against your student or do it together.

A quick tip to point out to your student is to make good use of the "S." For example:

– fire, fires, mane, manes, fate, fates

1. Prepare a "Boggle" grid. The no preparation way is to draw it on the whiteboard and make sure students can see it well.

2. The teacher and student both try to make as many words as possible with 4+ letters. Or, work together on it. Do not use/repeat the same letter in a single square within a single word.

3. Add up points or play just for fun!

o	r	p	t	s	a
e	a	i	e	t	f
b	k	n	e	r	i
a	d	r	g	o	r
c	o	t	l	s	e
k	f	h	m	a	n

Some possible words from this board:

green, pink, rake, back, fire, fires, fast, road, rose, mane, manes (there are many others)

Bucket Lists

Time: 5-10 minutes

Level: Intermediate-Advanced

Materials Required: None

Talk about what a "bucket list" is. Give students about five minutes to create a list of three things they want to do, see, or accomplish before they die. The teacher can do the same. Discuss answers together.

Procedure:

1. Begin by asking your student if he/she has heard the term "bucket list." Discuss it together if unfamiliar with it.

2. Give the student about five minutes to create their own bucket list and the teacher can do the same.

3. Discuss together.

Comic Strip Challenge

Time: 5-10 minutes

Level: Intermediate-Advanced

Materials Required: Comic strip printouts

This is a fun warm-up that is great for those students who are a little bit introverted because it doesn't involve speaking but instead focuses on writing. The student can print out a simple comic strip with blank speech bubbles and then fill it in. It's best if you can find one that matches the topic for that day, such as emotions, hobbies, dating, etc. The teacher should make one too. Then compare strips together together.

Procedure:

1. The student prints out a comic strip paper with blank speech bubbles.

2. Have the student fill in the comic strip and the teacher can do the same.

3. Compare comic strips.

Fill out an Application Form

Time: 15+ minutes

Level: Intermediate-Advanced

Materials Required: Application form

During a teacher training course, my tutor mentioned that "writing" is not only writing essays. He said that we can get our students to practice writing just about anything and it would be useful. That comment changed my outlook on teaching writing, especially to beginners.

One simple thing that beginners can do is fill out an application form for a job. To find an application form, Google "sample job application form USA." Filling out an application form is a very practical activity. People have to fill them when they want to get a job, visa, or for traveling.

Procedure

1. Get you student to print off an application form from the Internet (send them a link for the specific one you have in mind).

2. Teach some application form vocabulary that you anticipate your student will have problems with, as well as tips for answering some questions.

3. The student can fill out the application form while you offer assistance and feedback.

Give a Reason

Time: 5-10 minutes

Level: Beginner-Intermediate

Materials Required: None

If you're teaching your students about conjunctions, try out this simple activity. Write some sentence starters on the board using "because." For example:

- I was late for school because _____.

- My mom was angry at my sister because _____.

- I failed the test because _____.

The student has to think of the most creative reasons they can to finish off the sentences.

Teaching Tip:

This activity also lends itself well to "so" sentences that deal with consequences. For example:

- I missed my bus so _____.

- I woke up late so _____.

Procedure:

1. Write some sentences on the board with "because," but leave the reason blank.

2. The student has to creatively give the reason to finish the sentence.

3. Check answers.

Haiku Activity

Time: 5-15 minutes

Level: Beginner-Intermediate

Materials Required: None

Depending on your student's L1, they may have difficulty with English syllables. This is one activity you can do to practice. Since the only real rule of writing a haiku is the syllable pattern (5-7-5), they are low stress for students, compared to other forms of poetry.

Begin by showing your student several haikus and pointing out the 5-7-5 structure. If he/she is a bit more advanced, you can increase the challenge by having him/her write about nature, the traditional theme of haikus

Then, the student can try their hand at writing one. This makes a nice homework activity too.

Teaching Tips:

I like to use this one as a humorous example:

Haikus are easy,

But sometimes they don't make sense.

Refrigerator

(Credit: Internet and T-shirts everywhere)

Procedure:

1. In advance, prepare a few example haikus to demonstrate the 5-7-5 syllable structure.

2. Have the student write their own haiku.

3. Check their work.

Make a Sentence

Time: 5 minutes

Level: Beginner-Intermediate

Materials Required: None, or worksheet/whiteboard/PowerPoint

To practice current or review vocabulary, have the student make 1-5 sentences.

No Materials Version: Have your student use the textbook (if using one in class) and choose a given number of words to make sentences.

Whiteboard/PowerPoint Version: Give the student a list of words to use all or some of.

Worksheet/PowerPoint Version: Fill-in-the-blank or multiple choice with a word bank.

Procedure:

Begin with a brief oral review of the vocabulary words you want the student to work with and elicit from the student what the words mean.

No Prep Version: Have the student take out their books and notebooks and tell him/her a number of sentences to make using those words. For example, "Turn to page 53, and choose three vocabulary words. In your notebook, write a new sentence using each word."

Whiteboard/PowerPoint Version: Either give the student a word list to choose from, or for lower level classes, several sentences with a word bank. Have the student write the complete sentences in their notebooks.

Part of Speech Review

Time: 5-10 minutes

Level: Beginner-Advanced

Materials Required: Worksheet/whiteboard/PowerPoint

Give the student several sentences and do one of the following: identify the part of speech of underlined words; circle (nouns/verbs/adjectives...); or add a word of the correct part of speech (fill in or multiple choice). Scaffold with an example of the activity done correctly as well as examples of the part of speech being focused on, such as a list of 5-6 nouns they know.

For an example of this activity, using possessive pronouns, check out: *www.eslspeaking.org/part-of-speech*.

Procedure:

1. In advance, prepare several sentences either on a worksheet or PowerPoint, or write

them on the whiteboard.

2. Give the student at least one example demonstrating how you would like the activity to be completed, for example, fill in the blank or circle the noun.

3. Begin the activity by eliciting from the student several examples of the given part of speech. Add to the list if necessary.

4. Give the student 2-5 minutes to complete the activity, depending on whether they need to write the sentences in their notebook or complete a worksheet.

5. Check answers.

Plan a Trip

Time: 20+ minutes

Level: Intermediate-Advanced

Materials Required: Information from the Internet

Plan a dream vacation in English together with your student! Instead of researching in the student's first language, use *Google* in English. In order to practice writing, keep notes only in English. Here's an example of how you might plan your trip using English. You can have your student add as little, or as much detail as you'd like. However, the point of the activity is to practice writing in point form which is useful when writing outlines for tests or essays.

Day 1: Monday, January 1

Fly Seoul (3pm) ----> Vancouver (7am)

Check in Hotel ABC, 123 Avenue

Rest, relax

Day 2: Tuesday, January 2

Stay at Hotel ABC

Tour Stanley Park

Eat at Pub XYZ dinner

Day 3: Wednesday, January 3

Check out Hotel ABC

Rent car Budget 123

Drive to Whistler

Rent skis shop ABC

Go Skiing

Lunch at ski lodge

Check in Hotel ABC Whistler

Bed early

Procedure:

1. Do some Internet research about a place that you and the student both want to go. It's helpful to specify the number of days. Suggest some helpful websites to have a look at (*Trip Advisor, Air BnB*, etc.).

2. Make a day-by-day itinerary of what the trip is going to look like.

Practice Writing Fluently

Time: 5 minutes/class

Level: High beginner-Advanced

Materials Required: Notebook

For speaking and writing, there are two main ways to evaluate it: fluency and accuracy. Fluency is how fast you are able to do it. Accuracy is how good your grammar and vocabulary are. It's more complicated than that, but that's the simplest explanation!

Most English writing classes and textbooks focus on accuracy. It's much easier for a book, or teacher to point out grammar and vocabulary errors than to teach someone to write quickly. However, it's important to work on both. The good news is that you can easily help your student with writing fluency.

The student needs a notebook that they'll use only for this purpose. Assign a topic for each class. For example, "My family," or, "Plans for the weekend," or, "Hopes for the future," or, "My favourite book." Then, have him/her write about that topic for five minutes without using a cell-phone and dictionary. Beginners may only be able to do it for three minutes. The goal is to write quickly. If the student doesn't know how to spell something, just guess. It doesn't matter in a fluency writing exercise.

This is the most important thing—the pen should NEVER stop moving. If the student can't think of anything, write this sentence, "I don't know what to write. I don't know what to write. I don't. . ." After two or three times, he/she will think of something else! If you see your student not writing, tell them to make sure that their pen doesn't stop moving.

Over time, you'll notice that writing speed increases. Remember that the goal is to write more quickly, not to write accurately. Your student can work on grammar, vocabulary and structure at other times.

Procedure:

1. The student gets a notebook specifically for fluent writing practice.

2. Assign a topic of the day and amount of time to write.

3. Both you and the student can write for that specified amount of time without a cell-phone or dictionary. The goal is to write quickly.

4. Pens should never stop moving! The student can write, "I don't know what to write" instead.

5. Track progress over time with a word count chart.

Punctuation/Capitalization

Time: 5-10 minutes

Level: High Beginner-Intermediate

Materials Required: Worksheet

Younger students and those whose first languages have different punctuation and/or capitalization rules than English need frequent practice in order to master correct usage. Give your student a worksheet with a reading passage that has several errors related to these things. Have him/her correct it, adding punctuation and capital letters as needed. For lower level and younger students, focus on one element at a time, such as the word "I" or using commas in a list. More advanced students can have a mix, but since this is a short activity, keep it to one correction per sentence. Make the activity easier with multiple-choice and the student can simply circle the correct answer.

Procedure:

1. In advance, prepare a worksheet with a reading passage that has several mistakes in it related to capitalization or punctuation. The difficulty depends on the level of the student.

2. Give the student at least one example demonstrating how you would like the activity to be completed, for example, adding commas to a list.

3. Give the student 2-5 minutes to complete the activity.

4. Check answers.

Reverse Writing

Time: 20 minutes

Level: Intermediate-Advanced

Materials Required: Comprehension questions

Does this sound familiar? Students read a passage and then have to answer comprehension questions, either through writing or speaking. However, if you want to make things more interesting and challenge your student, consider doing this reverse writing activity.

Tell your student that you have comprehension questions but no reading passage. They can be anything you want, but here's one quick example:

- What was Tom's job?

- What was the weather like that day?

- What didn't he want to do? Why?

- What surprising thing happened at the end?

Get the student to be creative and answer the questions in point form. Then, they can write a short story about what happened to Tom. Talk together about what they wrote and the teacher can try to answer the comprehension questions based on the story that the student wrote.

Procedure:

1. Prepare some typical comprehension questions like you'd have for a short story. Give them to the student and tell him/her that you don't have the story but he/she will need to make it up themselves.

2. The student answers the questions in point form, and then writes a short story.

3. The student reads their story to the teacher and the teacher attempts to answer the original comprehension questions.

Translation

Time: Variable

Level: Intermediate-Advanced

Materials Required: Passage to translate

Translating is often seen as kind of a dirty word in language learning (unless it is your intended career) but once students reach intermediate fluency, it can be useful. By this stage, they are probably pretty good at getting their point across on a variety of topics.

However, your students may find themselves becoming complacent. Since they can get their point across, they may not be as motivated to increase their vocabulary or use more complex grammatical structures. This is where translation can take writing to the next level.

When translating, you need to take the nuance of the original text into account. You aren't simply stating your ideas or opinions. You must choose the words which express the original meaning.

Procedure:

1. Choose a short article for your student to translate. Or he/she can choose their own.

2. The student reads the article carefully and makes a note of important words. Caution them against just starting with the first word and translating through to the end.

3. To start the translation, the student just uses those key words and phrases to recreate the article. With more practice, they can work on being more exact.

4. Check the translations.

But, Don't Translate Word for Word

I taught in South Korean universities for about 10 years. The best students were the ones who thought, talked, and wrote in English only. The weakest students were those that translated word for word between English and their first language. When you're listening, don't translate every single word into your first language. Listen to an entire sentence, or paragraph and then translate the main ideas, if necessary. Translating word for word is only helpful to remind you of how the same meaning is expressed differently between English and your first language.

What Do you Know about Apples?

Time: 5-10 minutes

Level: Beginner-Intermediate

Materials Required: None

In this writing activity, students have to think of all the true statements they know about a certain topic. For example, apples, cats, David Beckham, etc. For apples, students may come up with the following sentences:

- There's an English idiom, "An apple a day keeps the doctor away."

- An apple is a fruit.

- There are green apples.

- There are red apples.

- Apples are healthy.

Give your student an allotted time. I find that five minutes works well. They have to write down all the true sentences they can think of about the topic. The teacher can do the same. The, compare sentences at the end of that time.

Teaching Tip:

Mention to students that they should not write negative statements. For example, "An apple is not a vegetable." Unless you do this, you'll sometimes get twenty sentences with, "An apple is not a/an animal/vegetable/car/piece of clothing."

Procedure:

1. Set a topic (apples).

2. Both student and teacher write as many true, positive statements as they can about the topic in a certain amount of time and then compare.

Word of the Day

Time: 5 minutes

Level: Beginner-Advanced

Materials Required: Whiteboard/PowerPoint

I have frequently been required to either give my students a word, quote, or idiom of the day, outside of our usual textbook, but it's usually related to the textbook or a monthly theme. You can easily start a Word of the Day activity for your students, by giving them a single word each day from their textbook (but not a vocabulary word), current events or by having a theme for each month.

Write the word on the whiteboard or PowerPoint along with the definition, part of speech, and several example sentences. Have the student copy all of this in his/her notebook in a section for their Words of the Day. You can use the word as an exit ticket, have a weekly quiz, or add one or two words to each regular vocabulary quiz.

Variation (more advanced): Idiom of the Day is where you give the student an idiom with a definition and a picture (if possible). Have him/her make 1-3 sentences using it correctly.

Procedure:

1. In advance, prepare a collection of words from your student's textbook but not part of the vocabulary list.

2. Begin each day (or one day per week) with one new word. Introduce the word just as you would their regular vocabulary: present the word, the definition, part of speech and

several example sentences.

3. Have the student copy the sentences in the notebooks and add their own sentence.

4. Add all or some Words of the Day to your regular vocabulary quizzes.

Word Poem/Name Poem

Time: 10-20 minutes

Level: Intermediate-Advanced

Materials Required: Example poem poster/PowerPoint

Here's another activity you undoubtedly did yourself as a student. Either give your student a word related to the lesson, or have them use their names (a great ice breaker activity). Begin each line with a letter from the word so that the first letter of each line read vertically spells the word. Using that letter, write a word or phrase that describes the word. Here's an example word poem: *www.eslspeaking.org/word-poem.*

Procedure:

1. In advance, prepare your own name or word poem to display for the student.

2. Show that the first letter of each line spells a word.

3. Give the student a word related to your lesson or have them use their names to make their own poem.

Words in Words

Time: 5 minutes

Level: Beginner-Advanced

Materials Required: None

You probably did this when you were in school. Assign a word and the teacher and student can work together to come up with as many words as possible based on it. For example: "vacation" = a, on, no, act, action, taco, ant, van, etc.

Wordles.com has a tool that allows you to type in a word and get the possible words. For vacation, they listed 45 words, some of which I should have thought of myself and some of which are "Scrabble words." Since your student will not possibly know all of these words, it is up to you whether you show all the answers or an abridged list.

Procedure:

1. Choose a long word.

2. Set a time limit.

3. Work together to make an many new words as possible.

4. When the activity is finished, show your student all of the possible words they could have made. You can get these from *www.wordles.com.*

Write an Email

Time: 30+ minutes

Level: Intermediate-Advanced

Materials Required: Example emails

Remember that writing is more than just a five-paragraph essay! It can include writing down some words in any form, whether long or short. So, why not get your student to work on writing an email in your class?

Email is quite a specific form of communication that has a few unwritten rules. If you follow them, the emails you send will be effective. If you don't, people probably won't read them!

The first tip I give my students is to keep emails brief, and direct. People get a lot of emails, especially at work. Make sure your emails are to the point! Make them very clear and easy to understand. Use simple grammar and vocabulary. The tone of your email should be polite, and not demanding.

Next, make sure you have a good subject line. By "good," we mean that it describes exactly what the email is about. For example, saying something like, "Hello friend," when your email is about an upcoming work meeting is bad! A better subject line would be, "Team A lunch meeting Jan. 2, 12:00."

Finally, don't forget to proofread. Read emails out loud at least once, checking for things like basic grammatical errors, spelling, etc.

Procedure:

1. Shown your student some example emails.

2. Give some tips about writing them. For example, choose a good subject line and keep it brief.

3. Give your student a reason to write an email (upcoming work meeting, hosting a party, etc.) and they can write one. Check answers.

Warm-Ups and Icebreakers

I usually start all my classes with a warm-up because it helps ease students into using English again before we jump into the heart of the lesson. I also like to use some icebreakers in the first class to help the student and I get to know each other and create a friendlier atmosphere. Here are some of the things that I like to do for those purposes.

Categories

Time: 5 minutes

Level: Beginner-Intermediate

Materials Required: None

Try out this quick vocabulary activity that requires nothing in the way of preparation or materials if you do it by speaking. If you have pen and paper, it's a nice writing activity as well.

The student can review by brainstorming words they know in a given category, such as food, job, hobbies, etc. I often use it as a warm-up if I know that my student has studied the topic I'm planning on teaching already. It's a nice way to activate prior knowledge about a topic.

A variation is to turn it into a friendly competition between the teacher and the student. Take turns saying one word from the category and keep going until someone can't name one that hasn't been said already.

Procedure:

1. For a speaking & listening activity, the student and teacher take turns adding a word related to a certain category by saying it out loud. If someone can't add a word that's not a repeat of what's already been said, the game is over.

2. For a written activity, give a time limit of around three minutes to brainstorm and write as many words that match the category as possible. The teacher can work together with the student, or the student can do it alone.

Deserted Island

Time: 5-10 minutes

Level: Beginner-Advanced

Materials Required: None

Deserted Island is an excellent way to uncover what things are most important to your student. Tell the student that there is a terrible storm and their ship is sinking, but thankfully, they can bring three objects with them. It doesn't need to be realistic or necessary for survival, just something that he/she wants to have with them during their time on the island. Encourage creativity and imagination.

The teacher can make their own list. Then, compare answers and discuss together.

Procedure:

1. Tell the student that they are on a ship and it's sinking. Thankfully, there is an island nearby that is already well-stocked with everything they'll need for survival.

2. The student has to choose three things to have with them during their time on the island. It doesn't need to be realistic or necessary for survival. The teacher can choose three objects as well.

3. Share and discuss answers.

Draw a Picture, but Someone Else is Talking

Time: 5-10 minutes

Level: Intermediate-Advanced

Materials Required: Blank paper

This is a fun way to practice body parts or descriptive words (big, small, long, etc.) and I guarantee that everyone will be laughing throughout this activity. The person talking describes something that they're looking at to their partner (a face, a body, a city, a monster) and that person draws what they hear. The results are usually hilarious.

For online teaching, it's easy for you to choose something to describe. For the student, I ask them to go to *Google Images* and search for "cartoon monster" or "cartoon alien" and then choose one of the pictures to describe to me.

Teaching Tips:

Some useful functional language that you can practice with this activity is asking for clarification. You can pre-teach some language surrounding the topic, such as:

How _____ (long, tall, etc.)?

What do you mean?

I didn't understand, could you say it again?

What did you say? I couldn't hear you.

Procedure:

1. Both the teacher and student choose a secret picture from *Google Images* or similar website.

2. The teacher describes what they see and the student draws it. Then, compare the drawing with the original.

3. Switch roles and do it again.

Fortunately, Unfortunately/Luckily, Unluckily

Time: 5 minutes

Level: Intermediate-Advanced

Materials Required: None

You may have played this game at school yourself. Start off by telling your student some good news (something that "happened to you") followed by some bad news. For example, "Unfortunately, my car wouldn't start this morning. Fortunately, my neighbor gave me a ride to school. Unfortunately, she drove through a red light. Fortunately . . ." Then, take turns adding one element of the story at a time, changing it from good news to bad and back as they go around their circle.

Procedure:

1. Start off with a couple examples (something that "happened to you"), alternating between good and bad news (example: see above).

2. With the student, take turns adding one element at a time. Each addition should change the story from good to bad or vice versa.

I'm Going on a Picnic

Time: 5-10 minutes

Level: Beginner-Advanced

Materials Required: None

This is an oldie, but a goodie. It gets students talking and thinking critically. Think of a rule for items on the picnic, but don't tell the student. For example, "must contain the letter E," or, "must be countable." Tell him/her that you are going on a picnic, and give examples of 3-5 items you are taking with you to give hints about your rule. Then, elicit from the student what he/she would take. If their item doesn't fit your rule, tell them that they can't come!

Once the student figures out the rule, switch roles and play again.

Procedure:

1. Think of a rule for items which can go on the picnic, such as "must contain the letter E," or, "must be countable."

2. Tell the student you are going on a picnic, and give examples of 3-5 items you are taking with you, to give them hints about your rule.

3. Elicit from the student what they would take. If their item doesn't fit your rule, tell them they can't take it.

4. Continue until the students figures out the rule.

5. Switch roles.

Mixed Up Sentences

Time: 5-10 minutes

Level: Beginner-Intermediate

Materials Required: None

Mixed up sentences is one of my favourite ways to review English grammar. I generally use it as a quick warm-up at the beginning of a class to review material from previous classes. It works well for beginner to intermediate level students of all ages. For advanced level students, it's far more difficult to make mixed up sentences without totally obvious mistakes that they'll pick up very, very easily.

For beginners and children, you may want to mix things up at the word level and have them make sentences by writing. However, for older, or more advanced level students, they can make a dialogue or story out of pre-made sentences.

Here's how to do it. Put up a "Mixed-Up" conversation or a few unrelated sentences on the board or in a PowerPoint presentation. The the student has to turn them into coherent English.

Teaching Tips:

If your goal is to practice specific grammar points, it will probably be faster to make your own dialogue or sentences than to repurpose one from the book.

However, if your students are beginners or high beginners, simply arranging a set of sentences in the correct order of a conversation may be challenging. In that case, you can save yourself some time by recycling a textbook dialogue which you covered several weeks or months earlier.

Procedure:

1. In advance, prepare a conversation using familiar vocabulary, or take a dialogue from a previous, but not too recent, lesson. Randomly arrange the sentences, or parts of sentences, if you want to make it more challenging. For the highest level students, you could have them do both. First, arrange the sentences and then put them in some sort of order to make a coherent conversation.

2. The student correctly arranges the sentences or words within the sentences.

3. Check answers.

My World

Time: 10-15 minutes

Level: Beginner-Intermediate

Materials Required: None

This is an excellent icebreaker activity that you can do on the first day of class to help get to know each other. Start by drawing a big circle on the whiteboard with the title, "My World." Inside the circle there are various words, pictures or numbers that have some meaning to you.

For example, inside my circle there might be 1979, blue, 37, a picture of two cats, and a mountain. The student would then have to make some guesses about why these things are special to me. The correct answers are: my birth year, favorite color, number of countries I've been to, my pets, and hiking which is my favorite hobby.

The student can make their own world and you can make some guesses about what the things are.

Teaching Tips:

This is a good activity to practice some functional language dealing with correct or incorrect guesses. Teach your students how to say things like, "You're close," "Almost," "You got it," "That's right," and "Really? No!"

For beginners, this activity might be a bit of challenge. You could write down these question forms to help them out:

Is this your _____ (hobby, birth year, age, favorite color)?

*Do you have */a/an _____ (cat, three family members, etc.)?*

Have you _____ (visited, gone to, tried, etc.)?

Procedure:

1. Draw a big circle on the board and write "My World" at the top. Put in some words, pictures or numbers inside the circle that have some meaning to you. Have the student make some guesses about what the things mean.

2. Have the student prepare their own "world." I usually allow around three minutes to do this. Make some guesses about the items that the students has in their world.

Name Five Things

Time: 5 minutes

Level: Beginner-Intermediate

Materials Required: None

This is an excellent warm-up activity to review vocabulary words from the previous class.Tell the students to name five _____. The category will depend on the level and age of students.

For beginners, you could do easy things like animals, colors, fruits, etc. For higher level students, you could use things that move, animals with four legs, things that can fly, breakfast foods, etc.

It can be either a speaking or a writing activity.

Procedure:

1. Tell the student to name five _____.

2. Repeat as many times as you'd like.

Odd One Out

Time: 5 minutes

Level: Beginner-Advanced

Materials Required: Groups of words

You can use Odd One Out to review vocabulary from the previous classes. Write up a few sets of vocabulary words on the board. I use four in one group, with one of them being the odd one out. For example, orange, yellow, apple, banana. Yellow is the odd one out because it's not a fruit.

Procedure:

1. Make 4-6 groups of 4 words, with one of them being unlike the others.

2. The student has to choose the odd word from each group and also write (or say) why they chose it. Example: Yellow—not a fruit.

Phone Show and Tell

Time: 5 minutes

Level: Beginner-Advanced

Materials Required: Image from the student's phone as well as yours.

Both the teacher and student choose an interesting picture from their phones and talk about it together. This can lead to many interesting conversations and is an excellent way to get to know each other.

Sentence Substitution Ladder

Time: 5-20 minutes

Level: Beginner-Intermediate

Materials Required: Sentences

This is a simple activity to get students to think about how they can use the words they know. They will be very familiar with substitution drills, but this goes a step further to get lower level students comfortable with using the language a bit more creatively. They have the knowledge, but they may need a push to use it.

Give the student a sentence practicing familiar categories of words (places, activities, etc.) and a familiar grammatical structure by writing it on the whiteboard.

Then, instruct the student to change one word at a time to make a new sentence. Each position must be changed one time (first word, second word, etc.), but it doesn't have to be done in order.

The student can do this by writing new sentences in their notebook (3-5 is a good number to aim for).

An example ladder would be:

Original sentence: I saw a black cat walk under a ladder.

I saw an orange cat walk under a ladder.

We saw an orange cat walk under a ladder.

We saw an orange cat run under a ladder.

We saw an orange cat run under the bed.

We saw an orange cat run to the bed.

We heard an orange cat run to the bed.

We heard an orange dog run to the bed.

Teaching Tip:

Unless you want to specifically target articles and numbers, consider noun phrases as a single unit.

Procedure:

1. In advance, prepare several sentences using familiar categories of words (places, activities, etc.) and a familiar grammatical structure. You can also do this on the spot if you have no preparation time.

2. Have the student change one word at a time to make a new sentence.

Would You Rather?

Time: 5-10 minutes

Level: Beginner-Advanced

Materials Required: None

Would You Rather? is a fun ESL warm-up activity. You can buy ready-made decks, but they aren't ESL specific. I use self-made cards, which takes a bit of time but then you can recycle them from class to class. Another option is to make a list of questions. If you're quick on your feet, you can do this without materials. The student can think of some questions too.

For example, "Would you rather have eyes like a fly's, or eyes like a spider's?" Each of you must answer the question and explain why.

Procedure:

1. In advance, prepare questions, the odder, the better. For example, "Would you rather have eyes like a fly's, or eyes like a spider's?" It's also possible to do this on the spot.

2. Discuss which option each of you would choose and why.

Multi-Skill Activities

Activities that involve more than one skill are kind of the holy grail of English teaching and I love to include them in my lessons. You probably do too I'm sure! Check out some of my favourite activities and games that cover a range of skills.

2 Truths and a Lie

Skills: Writing/Listening/Speaking

Time: 20-30 minutes

Level: Intermediate-Advanced

Materials Required: None

This is the perfect icebreaker activity that requires large amounts of speaking and listening. The best part is that it requires no prep whatsoever and not even paper or a whiteboard, unless you want to have students write down their three sentences instead of just remembering them in their heads.

Both you and the student write three sentences, one of which is false. Then, read the sentences and the other person guesses the false one. Higher level classes can ask three questions or question the person for a pre-determined amount of time (two minutes) to determine the false one.

Teaching Tips:

This is a useful activity for practicing the speaking sub-skills of initiating a conversation and responding to something in a questioning way. For example, students might say, "So you can make/play/do _____? I kind of don't believe you! Tell me _____" if you allow question or response time.

Emphasize that students must pick things that are "big picture" ideas. The terrible examples I give are things like birthdays, hospital they were born in, name of sister, etc. There is simply no way to verify this information through asking any sort of interesting questions. Better categories are things like hobbies, travel, part-time jobs, skills and abilities. I have students write down their statements and try to catch any of the bad ones before the game starts. Of course, they shouldn't indicate whether they are true or false when you're checking them so that you can play too!

Procedure:

1. Write three sentences on the board about yourself: two are true and one is not. Or, just say your three sentences slowly out loud.

2. Explain to the student that they are to do the same for themselves.

3. Choose which statement from the other person is false. It makes it more interesting to have a question period first.

English Central

Skills: Listening/Speaking

Time: 10-15 minutes

Level: Beginner-Advanced

Materials Required: Internet connection

English Central is YouTube for language learners. There is premium content and functionality, but you can enjoy many features for free. YouTube has subtitles on some videos, but English Central takes it to the next level. The videos have been curated and organized by level, topic, and/or language skill and each video is segmented for easy replay of a chunk of speech. Students can also click on a single word to hear it pronounced slowly and clearly.

One activity you can use English Central for is pronunciation. Have your student listen to a clip and repeat. The videos for young learners are fairly simple, with slow, and clear speech. You can pause after each phrase or sentence and repeat as needed.

Begin by playing the entire clip once or twice. Then, replay the clip bit by bit for the student to repeat. Each clip is a short story, so you can also watch and discuss and/or summarize a clip as a 90-60-30 fluency activity.

Teaching Tips:

You can sign in with Facebook, but it would be better to set up a free account in your student's name.

Procedure:

1. Make sure you will have an internet connection.
2. Select a video in advance or let your student choose one. There are "courses" which are sets of related videos, which you can work through in a series.
3. Play the entire clip once or twice.
4. Play one segment (sentence or phrase) at a time and have the student repeat, trying to copy the pronunciation.
5. End by watching the entire clip one more time and discussing and/ or summarizing.

Finish the Sentence

Skills: Listening/Writing

Time: 5-10 minutes

Level: Beginner-Intermediate

Materials Required: None

This is a simple activity that can be used for any grammar point that you're teaching. It's partly listening/dictation practice and partly a writing activity.

The way it works is that you think of a few sentence starters related to whatever you're teaching. Or, you can use it as a review activity for things covered in previous classes. For example:

"If I were you, _____."

"Despite the cool weather, _____."

"I wish he/she _____."

Say them to your student who has to write them down. Then, give him/her time to finish the sentences in a grammatically correct way. As you can see, they lend themselves to any and all grammatical constructions.

Procedure:

1. Think of some sentence starters related to your target grammar.

2. Dictate them one by one to your student who writes them down in their notebook.

3. Then he/shes finishes the sentences in a grammatically correct way.

4. Check for errors.

Is That Sentence Correct?

Skills: Listening/Speaking/Writing

Time: 5-10 minutes

Level: Beginner-Advanced

Materials Required: Blank paper, vocabulary words

"Is that Sentence Correct?" is an English grammar activity. Make a worksheets with some sentences. Some of them are correct while others are not. The student reads the sentences and discusses whether they are correct or not. Continue until all the sentences are finished.

Procedure:

1. Prepare a worksheet with a mix of correct and incorrect sentences.

2. The student reads the sentences and decides whether or not they are correct.

3. If incorrect, the student should explain why.

New Language Pile Up

Skills: Reading/Writing/Listening/Speaking

Time: 5 minutes at the beginning and end of class

Level: Beginner-Advanced

Materials Required: Index cards, pen

One benefit of one-on-one lessons is that you can help your student create a personalized set of flashcards, rather than just an ongoing set of new vocabulary lists. Throughout each lesson, each time the student comes across an unfamiliar word or phrase, make note of it on a blank index card. Wrap lessons up by going through each card, explaining the word/ phrase and giving the student an additional example or two of use in context.

For homework, have the student look the words up in the dictionary and make their own sentences so you can check for comprehension the following lesson. You can begin with a review of the previous terms before moving on to new material. If you want to take it to the next level, have the student email you their sentences, so you have your own record of which terms they are working on. This way you can prepare periodic lessons to focus on and recycle the Pile Up.

Procedure:

1. Bring a pen and blank index cards to each lesson (or have the student bring them).

2. Begin each lesson by reviewing the previous week's words.

3. Throughout your lesson, when your student encounters new terms, record one on each card.

4. Conclude the lesson by reviewing each term and providing additional examples of usage.

5. Assign looking up each word and writing an original sentence for homework.

Picture Prompt

Skills: Listening/Writing or Speaking

Time: 5 minutes

Level: Beginner-Advanced

Materials Required: A picture with people doing things

Picture prompt is a great ESL warm-up for kids as well as adults. It can be used for all levels from beginner to advanced. Show your student an image and have them generate questions or speculate about the picture. In particular, it works well if you're teaching your students about questions forms, transitions, relative clauses or adjectives.

Question Examples for Beginner Students

For lower level students, this can be purely descriptive:

Q: What do you see?

A: I see a house, a car, and some people.

Q: What colour is the car?

A: It is blue.

Question Examples for Intermediate Level Students

For high beginner/low intermediate students, have an image which can generate questions such as:

What is happening in this picture?

How does that person feel?

Why do you think so?

Or, you may also use it to focus on English prepositions. For example:

Where is the book?

Is the man standing next to the child?

Example Questions for Advanced Students

For more advanced students, use an unusual image. Encourage them to create a narrative to explain the story. You could have students create a story about the picture in a few minutes. Or, you could have them write an explanation for what happened.

Teaching Tips:

You can find collections of unusual images online which are perfect for advanced students to create their narratives. Just search on Google Images or something similar according to your topic that day.

For beginners, you can either say the questions out loud and students have to answer them, or you could make a worksheet with room for students' answers.

If you have more advanced students in a writing class, more options are available to you for what you can do. You may even require students to write a paragraph, essay or a creative story based on the picture that you show them.

Procedure:

1. In advance, prepare an image, either PowerPoint or a picture.

2. Depending on the level of the student and the focus of your lesson you may do the following:

   – Elicit descriptive sentences about the image.

- Write down what is happening in the picture, how the person/people feel and why they think so, etc.

- Create a narrative about the image. Unusual images work well for this.

- Complete a worksheet of simple questions.

Quick Read

Skills: Reading/Writing/Speaking

Time: 10 minutes

Level: Beginner-Advanced

Materials Required: Worksheet

Give your student a short passage, slightly below their level, and 3-5 comprehension questions. It should be short enough to be completed in 7-8 minutes. This is a good way to recycle previous material by summarizing a story or part of a story. You can also use this as a pre-test before beginning a new lesson to gauge their existing knowledge of a topic or the relevant vocabulary

Procedure:

1. In advance, prepare a short passage using language slightly below the level of the class.
2. Include 3-5 comprehension questions and an example question demonstrating how to answer.
3. Give the student 7-8 minutes to read and answer the questions.

Test Prep: Speaking to Essay Writing

Skills: Writing/Speaking

Time: 40-60 minutes

Level: Intermediate-Advanced

Materials Required: Prepared writing prompts, timer (phone, kitchen timer, etc.)

If your student is planning to take a standardized test of English ability, he/she will need to prepare for the timed essay. The essay intimidates many students, but as long as they practice the expected format with the main categories of prompts (choose a side, explain or describe, and compare advantages and disadvantages), they don't need to be worried. One way to ease your students into essay writing is by using the prompt as a guided speaking activity to help them brainstorm and fully develop some ideas and opinions.

Once your student has a good idea on where he/she stands on a given topic, it's time to put pen to paper. I also remind my student that there is no lie detector: if they have an opinion based on one strong reason, but the opposite opinion has numerous weaker reasons, then it's best to defend the easier position. Start by introducing some important language such as linking words and phrases and opinion words and phrases.

Some examples of these are:

In my opinion,

On the other hand,

I think/feel/believe _____.

Some people think/feel/believe _____, but I disagree.

I'm convinced/sure/certain/positive _____.

Some would say/argue _____, but to me. . .

Once you have gone over these, give the student a prompt. He/she can answer the question with one sentence. For an opinion prompt, try to get the student to give three or four reasons and then have them explain or give examples to back up those reasons. The more reasons the better because once your student starts writing, the focus can be on the ones that provide the best examples.

Finally, ask the student about the opposing opinion. Why do some people have that opinion? For choose-a-side prompts, addressing the opposing position is a good topic for the third body paragraph.

Once you've talked through the essay with the student, it is time to write. This is ideal to do as a homework exercise before the next class.

Procedure:

1. In advance, prepare a writing prompt of the style used in standardized tests (choose a side, explain or describe, and compare advantages and disadvantages) and a timer.

2. Start by introducing some important language such as linking words and phrases and opinion words and phrases. Some examples of these are listed above.

3. Give the student a prompt.

4. Instruct him/her to each answer the question with one sentence. Then, ask the student to expand on their answer by giving more reasons or details.

5. Once the student has given several reasons and examples, talk about the opposing opinion.

6. Assign the essay for homework.

Text Me!

Skills: Reading/Writing

Time: 5-10 minutes

Level: Beginner-Intermediate

Materials Required: Paper and pens or two phones

If you and your student need a break from speaking, conduct a lesson (or part of one) via text message. Texting is quite different from other forms of written English, so if your student is likely to need to communicate by text in English, introduce them to "text speak" (common abbreviations) as well as common emoticons as they are different in different cultures.

Pretend you are conducting the lesson from a distance. Write tasks for your student and encourage them to write you any questions. Communicate via short notes while your student works.

Teaching Tip:

You can provide subtle correction by demonstrating correct usage of any vocabulary or grammar they misuse in your replies, or by doing some talking throughout the activity.

Procedure:

1. Briefly write a task for your student to complete without speaking. Specifically request they ask you (in writing) any questions they have about the task while they are working.

2. Communicate back and forth in brief messages to one another.

What are you Cooking?

Skills: Writing/Speaking/Listening/Reading

Time: 15 minutes

Level: Intermediate-Advanced

Materials Required: None

Both you and your student can write down items from each of the following categories:

- 1 meat

- 1 dairy product

- 1 green vegetable

- 3 more vegetables

- 1 grain

- 3 fruits

- 1 tin of some kind of food

- 1 jar of some food

- something salty

- something sweet

- 3 herbs or spices

Then, trade papers. Explain what a three course meal is and give the student some examples. You could use *Google Image* search and look for "three course meal." There are lots of nice examples there.

Each person has 5-10 minutes to plan a three course meal with their ingredients, along with cooking oil, salt and pepper. However, they are not required to use all the ingredients if they don't want to. It should consist of an appetizer, main course, and dessert.

When each person is finished, they can share their menu with the other.

Procedure:

1. Both teacher and student write down the required ingredients in each category. This usually takes around five minutes.

2. Trade papers.

3. Each person must make a three course menu with their ingredients (appetizer, main course and dessert). They don't have to use all the ingredients.

4. Share the 3-course menu with the other person.

Where Are They Now?

Skills: Speaking/Writing/Reading

Time: 10-15 minutes

Level: Beginner-Advanced

Materials Required: None

This is a post-reading extension activity that can be done orally or in writing. When you finish a novel or story, have the student imagine the main character five or ten years in the future. Where are they? What are they doing? How have the events in the story affected his/her life?

Teaching Tip:

If your student has difficulty, help them with brainstorming. Show him/her how to make a mind map with items such as: relationship, job, hobbies, home, pet, etc. Talk with your student about how his or her own life has changed in the past five or ten years.

Procedure:

1. After reading a story or novel, discuss how the character changed over the course of the story and why.

2. Have your student write or discuss what he/she thinks the character's life is like five or ten years in the future.

Resources

For planning ESL/EFL lessons, there are so many resources out there. Here are some of the best ones that I use regularly.

Boggles World

If you teach English online to kids, then certainly have a look at *Boggles World* (*www.bogglesworldesl.com*). There are lesson plans, worksheets, flashcards, crosswords and a whole lot more. The best part? It's all free.

Breaking News English

If you're an English teacher, whether online or in the classroom, you're going to need *Breaking News English* (*www.breakingnewsenglish.com*). It's some serious English teaching gold and one of the top options for reading and listening passages. They come in a variety of different levels too.

Not just that though. All of that material comes along with entire lesson plans that you can literally just print off and take to class. There are full lesson plans along with smaller, mini-lessons for shorter classes. It really is that easy to have better online ESL classes if you check out this site.

British Council Learning English

The British Council (*www.learnenglish.britishcouncil.org*) has some excellent lesson planning resources. This section of the website is designed for English learners and it is certainly possible for students to use this for independent study. However, there is lots of good stuff there to use in classes as well, covering all the skills and other things too like business English.

Business English Pod

If you teach business English online, then this should be your #1 stop! *Business English Pod* (*www.businessenglishpod.com*)is heavy on the listening but covers all the other skills reasonably well and focuses on things that business students will find relevant. For example, telephone conversations, negotiations, writing emails, etc.

There is a paid version of this site but in general, I've found that the free version is useful enough for my needs. However, if you teach online business English exclusively, then consider the upgrade.

Busy Teacher

Another great source of worksheets and lesson plans is *Busy Teacher* (*www.busyteacher.org*). They specialize in worksheets but also have a number of lesson plans. I also like to use their puzzle makers as well.

ESL Library

Although it's a paid site, *ESL Library* (*https://www.esllibrary.com*) is so good that it's worth paying for! Their lessons plans are interesting, engaging and contain everything you need to have some great online classes with your students. Additional preparation time is minimal.

Besides the 1000+ lessons plans, they have flashcards, images, resources, digital activities, homework and reporting tools. Basically, everything an online teacher needs if they're serious about helping students make some improvements in their English skills.

ESL Textbooks

There are three schools of thought when it comes to teaching English online:

- Use materials provided by the platform you're working on (sometimes mandatory)

- Piece together materials from various websites and books

- Follow an ESL textbook from start to finish

The third option certainly has some merit if the student's goal is to improve their general English ability and not for some very specific purpose. This is because following through a textbook series will cover new grammar and vocabulary in an organized fashion and also provide lots of opportunity for practicing a variety of skills.

Some good textbook recommendations include the following:

- *4 Corners, Smart Choice, Touchstone, World Link, Interchange* (4-skills)

- *Market Leader* (Business English)

- *Great Writing* (writing)

Film English

If your student is into movies, then you may want to check out *Film English* (*www.film-english.com*) when planning your ESL online classes. There is a wealth of material here and it would be easy to plan an entire course based on this website!

Not only are the movie choices interesting and suitable for a variety of different levels but the lesson plans are robust and contain a variety of different exercises.

ISL Collective

The main reason to consider checking out *ISL Collective* (*www.en.islcollective.com*) is the worksheets. There are so many of them for just about any grammar point you can possibly imagine. Use them for homework for your students as it's a real time-saver to not have to make your own.

Besides that, they have a number of excellent lesson plans as well and just about anything an English teacher needs to get started, including PowerPoints and video lessons.

Puzzle Maker

I love to make some puzzles for my students as a way to review grammar or vocabulary. One of the best places to make them is at this site (*www.puzzlemaker.discoveryeducation.com*). It does take a little bit of time to figure out the ins and outs of how to do it, but after that, it's simple to make one in just a few minutes.

Before You Go

If you found this book useful, please head on over to Amazon and leave a review. It will help other teachers like you find the book. Also be sure to check out my other books on *Amazon* at *www.amazon.com/author/jackiebolen.*There are plenty more ESL activities and games for children as well as adults. Here are some of the most popular titles:

39 No-Prep/Low-Prep ESL Speaking Activities

39 ESL Icebreakers

39 Awesome 1-1 ESL Activities

101 ESL Activities

Life After ESL: Foreign Teachers Returning Home

CPSIA information can be obtained
at www.ICGtesting.com
Printed in the USA
LVHW101558290121
677703LV00013B/134